IRA AND 401(K) INVESTMENT IN REAL ESTATE

for Syndicators,
Other Real Estate Professionals,
and the Rest of Us

STEPHEN L. SMITH

iUniverse, Inc.
Bloomington

IRA and 401(k) Investment in Real Estate for Syndicators,
Other Real Estate Professionals, and the Rest of Us

iUniverse books may be ordered through booksellers or by contacting:

iUniverse
1663 Liberty Drive
Bloomington, IN 47403
www.iuniverse.com
1-800-Authors (1-800-288-4677)

ISBN: 978-1-4502-9962-6 (pbk)
ISBN: 978-1-4502-9964-0 (cloth)
ISBN: 978-1-4502-9963-3 (ebk)

Library of Congress Control Number: 2011904974

Printed in the United States of America

iUniverse rev. date: 3/31/2011

Acknowledgments

I want to thank the many people who helped me get interested in IRA and 401(k) investments in real estate. I first want to thank my wife, Debra, for persevering through the many hours while I worked on this book. I particularly want to thank my secretary, Brooks Sibley, for keeping a good disposition through the many edits of this book. I also want to thank Andrea Cooper for helping edit the book.

Front Cover Photographs

Photograph of mountains are of Wild Mountain, Buncombe County, North Carolina. The photograph was taken by Jeff Zimmerman and commissioned by David LaFave. Photograph of condominium in Key West, Florida, taken by Debra T. Smith.

WARNING AND DISCLAIMER

The rules related to IRA and 401(k) investment are among the most complex in the federal tax law area. On top of the tax laws are layered the rules of ERISA (Employee Retirement Income Security Act of 1974) and Department of Labor pronouncements. As you will see from even a cursory examination of this book, even the so-called experts do not always seem to agree on exactly what the rules are. This is perfectly understandable because the IRS seems to change the rules constantly. On top of the IRS rules, you are also dealing with compliance officers who sometimes have rules that go beyond what I might think even the IRS requires.

This book is intended to provide general information regarding the tax and other laws applicable to IRA and 401(k) investment in alternative investments, particularly real estate. It is not intended as a substitute for the practitioner's own research, or for the advice of a qualified specialist. The author and publisher shall have neither liability nor responsibility to any person or entity with respect to any loss or damage caused, or alleged to be caused, directly or indirectly by the information contained in this book.

Please visit realestateinira.com for corrections or additions to this book.

CONTENTS

About The Author

Stephen L. Smith has more than 30 years experience in tax planning. He combines a strong academic background with practical application of this knowledge to individual circumstances. He earned his bachelors degree from UNC Chapel Hill, where he graduated Phi Beta Kappa. He attended the University of Virginia Law School where he was inducted into the prestigious Order of the Coif. He has addressed numerous business and industry groups on tax subjects specifically applicable to their unique circumstances.

The largest part of his day to day practice is working with people in the area of tax advantaged real estate transactions such as like-kind exchanges, real estate investments by IRAs and qualified plans and related areas, and estate planning. Steve practices law with the law firm of Horack, Talley, Pharr & Lowndes, P.A. where he has been a partner for over 25 years. He has written extensively in the areas of the taxation of IRAs, 401(k)s and other retirement plans investing in real estate and has been involved in seminars to other professionals on the subject of investing IRAs, 401(k)s and other self-directed plans in real estate investments. Steve has been involved in various real estate investments personally, including through his IRA and firmly believes in the value of real estate investment as a means of building wealth.

INTRODUCTION

WELCOME

I am delighted that you have decided to become interested in IRA investment in real estate. This book can help you take control of your own investments in a way that is just not possible through the stock market. You can legally invest in raw land or income-producing properties such as condominiums or shopping centers.

In addition to opening up the possibilities for some significant profits, you can invest in properties that are much more personal and real to you than some investment in a mutual fund. I cannot quantify the value of this but there is certainly something there that makes investment in real estate very attractive to many of us.

WHY I WROTE THIS BOOK

I am aware that there are other books that have been written regarding IRA investment in real estate and other non-traditional assets (traditional assets in my mind are stocks, bonds and mutual funds invested in stocks and bonds). However, I have always felt that much of what is written avoids some of the difficult questions in interpreting the rules in this area. This book is intended to do that. You will see that there are areas where even the experts do not agree, but this book will at least highlight the areas where questions exist.

Also, I have never seen a book I thought adequately dealt with the peculiar concerns of syndicators and other real estate professionals. This book is intended to fill that void.

While I have tried to cover the particular concerns of syndicators and other real estate professionals, I think you will find this book will be of great help to those of you who are looking at possible investments in real estate through your IRAs yourselves. If you will follow the rules in this book and then seek professional help as needed, you should be able to navigate the myriad rules in this area. One thing I can tell you from personal experience is that taking charge of your investments through your IRAs and 401(k)s is very satisfying and can lead to far greater returns than is typically the case.

While this book undertakes to provide guidance on many difficult questions, I have intentionally tried to stick to the middle ground between not avoiding the issues and having a treatise unreadable for most people. There are whole volumes on subjects such as prohibited transactions, unrelated business taxable income, and the Plan Asset Rules. I have intentionally touched on the rules enough to tell you when you need to seek further guidance without getting you so bogged down in the rules that the book is worthless to you.

How I Became Interested

I have written this book because I have become very interested in this subject personally. I have been involved in IRA investment in real estate for many years. The way I became involved in this was that I had an opportunity to invest in some land in the Phoenix area. One of the parties dropped out at the last moment and a client of mine was looking for investors to be able to close on the purchase. We went into the transaction relatively sure that we could sell the property for twice what we were paying for it within a relatively short time.

The only problem with this investment was that I was reluctant to part with the amount of cash out of my bank account that it would take to make the investment. I could have made the investment on my own, but I chose not to.

I wanted to use the funds in my IRA to make up the difference between what I was willing to take out of my bank account and the total amount that I needed to make the investment. I talked to a stockbroker friend who had handled my IRA and my wife's IRA for years and he advised me that his company could not be involved in my intended investment in real estate.

I therefore turned to Entrust New Direction IRA. Entrust is one of a number of companies that allows for self-directed IRA investment. Entrust acts as the administrator for self-directed IRAs. While Entrust has a number of branches, I chose the one in Boulder, Colorado, for a number of reasons.

I then invested in this land together with my IRA and a number of other parties. Actually, we set up a limited liability company ("LLC") in which we all invested and which owned the land in Phoenix and then eventually the shopping center referred to below. We sold the land some 6 months later for approximately twice what we paid for it. We then did a like-kind exchange (not because of the IRA but because of the significant personal investment by the parties) into a small strip shopping center in the Goose Creek, South Carolina area outside of Charleston. My IRA and I still own interests in this LLC. A like-kind exchange is a sale of real property followed by a purchase of replacement real property which can allow for the gain on the original sale to be deferred as long as the transaction meets specific IRS rules.

While I experienced unusual good fortune in this investment, this should give you some idea of what can be done with the opportunities that await you in the world of IRA investment in real estate. I have recently purchased a condominium unit for investment in my IRA and my wife's 401(k). Because of the low loan rates, we partnered with our IRA and 401(k). Partnering is discussed later in this book but essentially, it involves you investing along with your IRA or 401(k), usually with borrowed funds. The challenge here is that you cannot use the IRA or the property purchased by the IRA as security for the loan.

WHY THIS BOOK SHOULD BE OF INTEREST

There is currently an unprecedented opportunity for people to convert existing IRAs to Roth IRAs. This can allow you (at a current tax cost) to receive tax free distributions in the future. This ability to use the Roth IRA had not been available to people with significant adjusted gross incomes (exceeding $100,000), so the Roth IRA was not previously available to a great many people. Obviously, the Roth IRA is now of interest to a much larger group of people holding IRAs.

This book should also be of interest because it can open up a world of investments in real estate. Given the uncertainties faced in the stock market and with social security as well as the evaporation of the pension plan, you should be particularly interested in anything that allows you to take control of your retirement investments yourself.

Syndicators and other real estate professionals should be interested for a number of reasons. The main one is the fact that there are many opportunities for investment in real estate out there during this period when real estate prices have been driven down during the recession. There is a great deal of investment capital out there in IRAs.

Brokers and real estate agents should be interested because they are going to get questions regarding IRA investment in real estate and they have to be prepared to answer those questions. If those professionals are not prepared to answer these questions, then they will lose business to brokers and real estate agents who can answer the questions. The significant investment capital in IRAs provides a source of capital for investment in real estate that will generate commissions for the savvy broker or Realtor.

While many sections of this book refer to IRA investment in real estate, many of the same principles apply to investment by 401(k)s in real estate. There are, however, some specific differences in the 401(k)s that are also touched upon later but generally a 401(k) can invest in real estate the same way an IRA can.

Conclusion

Read and equip yourself to take charge of the significant funds in your IRAs and 401(k) accounts so that you can invest them in real estate if you so choose. I think you will find this knowledge both useful in building your personal wealth as well as empowering in enabling you to further take charge of your own investments.

CHAPTER 1

Background on the IRA
(as Well as Some Background on the 401(k) Plan)

INTRODUCTION

Before turning to why this is such a hot topic now and to why you and real estate professionals should be interested in this topic, I thought it best to give you some background on the nature of an IRA so you will know what I am talking about. My purpose is not to get you bogged down in information about IRAs but to give you enough information to navigate the balance of this book. If you will take a few minutes to familiarize yourself with what an IRA is and is not, it may help you as you read the rest of this book and focus in on investments in real estate which is our real interest. If you are already very familiar with IRAs, you have my permission to skim over this chapter to get right into the meat of this book, which is IRA investment in real estate.

WHAT IS AN IRA?

Some of the points below are discussed elsewhere in this book but a read through of this list will give the reader at least some idea of what an IRA is all about.

- An IRA or individual retirement account is a retirement vehicle that was set up under federal legislation to encourage those who do not have other retirement plans available to them to make contributions to an account from which withdrawals will be made by the owner during retirement.

- IRAs come in two main types, traditional and Roth. There are also spousal counterparts of both. More on this below.

- The contributions to a traditional IRA (as opposed to a Roth IRA) may be tax deductible, but are limited or eliminated in the case of employees who are covered under other types of retirement plans. The subject of contributions and distributions from an IRA will be dealt with in more detail later in this book.

- Contributions to Roth IRAs are not tax deductible.

- The trade off for the non-deductibility of contributions to a Roth IRA is that the distributions from the Roth are not taxable so the gains on any property you invest in a Roth IRA will escape further taxation. Like the traditional IRA, the contributions to a Roth are also limited or eliminated in the case of persons covered by other retirement plans.

- There is currently an unprecedented opportunity available for conversion of existing IRAs into Roth IRAs by those with higher adjusted gross incomes who currently have traditional IRAs.

- There is a substantial amount of money in IRAs, both in terms of amounts contributed by employees prior to the time other retirement plans became popular, as well as rollover IRAs. There is currently in excess of $3.7 trillion in IRAs. Rollovers into IRAs currently are the greatest source of additional growth of IRAs.

- In a rollover IRA, a person retiring from employment or whose employment is terminated (which is not uncommon in these turbulent times) can direct the assets of their account under the 401(k) plan previously maintained with their former employer to be rolled over into an IRA. Other than the source of the funds in the IRA, a rollover IRA is treated like any other IRA. Funds can also be rolled over to an existing IRA.

- The employee can roll over his or her funds to any IRA administrator he or she wishes, but one of the choices available is a self-directed IRA. Under a self-directed IRA, the owner of the IRA can direct the administrator of the IRA to invest in any allowable legal investment, including real estate. Moreover, there are opportunities for in-service distributions from 401(k) plans so that employees who remain employed may nonetheless roll out at least part of their 401(k) funds into a self-directed IRA.

- The IRA is a trusteed or custodial account set up in the United States for the exclusive benefit of the creator and his or her beneficiaries. The account is created by a written agreement and must be held by a trustee or custodian which must be a bank, savings and loan association, credit union, insurance company or any other entity which satisfies the Secretary of the Treasury's requirements.

- All of these entities are examined at least annually by whatever regulatory agency is responsible for their administration generally.

- Contributions generally must be in cash except for rollovers.

- The owner must be taking distributions by April 1 of the year following the year in which he reaches the age of 70½. (This provision does not apply to Roth IRAs at least so long as the owner is alive.)

- IRAs are not qualified plans. Qualified plans such as 401(k)s are covered by ERISA (the Employee Retirement Income Security Act of 1974), while IRAs generally are not.

IRA AS A SEPARATE ENTITY

Here's an important lesson to help you stay out of trouble as far as violating the prohibited transaction rules for your IRA. The IRA is separate from you. Your IRA is its own entity. Focus on the following chart to help you remember this important concept.

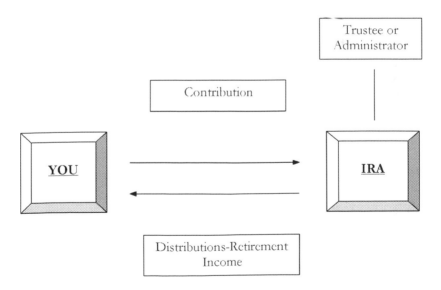

You cannot just treat your IRA as if it were your personal bank account and use it for your personal needs or you will end up entering into a prohibited transaction and causing the value of the IRA to be taxable to you. You could possibly even generate penalties if you are under age 59½.

If you learn nothing else from this book, make sure you take away the concept of the IRA as a separate entity from you.

TYPES OF INDIVIDUAL RETIREMENT ACCOUNTS

Now that you know what an IRA is, it may be helpful to summarize the types of IRAs that you are likely to encounter.

- Traditional. This is what has been the most typical type of IRA to which deductible contributions can be made. Deductions can be limited or eliminated if the owner is covered by some other form of retirement plan.

- Spousal Traditional. The traditional spousal IRA is really a misnomer since it is simply an IRA in the name of a spouse who has little or no income. This simply allows for a contribution to an IRA for the spouse based on the income of the working couple.

- Roth. As indicated, the key difference in the Roth IRA from the traditional IRA is that contributions are not deductible, but then distributions are not taxable. Again, there is a significant opportunity now for the conversion of traditional IRAs into Roth IRAs by owners of traditional IRAs having higher adjusted gross incomes.

- Spousal Roth. This is the counterpart of the spousal traditional IRA but has the features of a Roth IRA.

There are a number of other retirement accounts available including the Simplified Employee Pension ("SEP IRA"), the Savings Incentive Match Plan for Employees of Small Employers (SIMPLE) as well as qualified plan and 401(k) plans. The SEP IRA plan allows the employer to make contributions toward an employee's retirement by making contributions on behalf of the employee to a traditional IRA.

There are also two other types of accounts that operate under similar rules to IRAs. These are education savings accounts and health savings accounts. Contributions to these accounts may also be self-directed and the income on them is tax deferred.

WHAT IS A SELF-DIRECTED IRA?

The traditional IRA that you see opened through a bank or a mutual fund company allows a certain degree of self-direction in that the account holder can typically specify the investments, but only among the range of investments offered by that particular bank or mutual fund company. For

4

example, a bank typically allows for investment in certificates of deposit or other accounts with the bank as well as whatever selected family of mutual funds that bank approves of. If you are lucky, the bank allows for a reasonable selection of mutual funds.

The same is true of mutual fund companies. For example, if your IRA is with Merrill Lynch or Morgan Stanley, then typically Merrill Lynch or Morgan Stanley will offer their respective families of funds. Conversely, if you are with Charles Schwab or some other discount brokerage firm, then they will offer the various mutual funds that Charles Schwab offers. In either case, whether you are talking about a bank or a mutual fund company, your choices will be limited to the types of traditional investments that the banks and mutual fund companies usually deal with.

However, you are not legally limited to those types of investments and there are a number of companies that allow full self-direction that allows you to invest in anything which is legally permissible. The self-directed IRA administrator I have the most familiarity with is Entrust New Direction IRA. However, there are other legitimate self-directed IRA administrators as well. Pensco Trust Company is another one with a national reputation. There are doubtless other reputable administrators that offer self-directed IRAs.

Advantages of a Self-Directed IRA

A true self-directed IRA allows you much greater flexibility in terms of the types of assets that you invest in. This can allow you to greatly diversify your investment portfolio.

Let's go back to my example. I fell into the world of self-directed IRAs while investing in real estate when an investment opportunity came open in the Phoenix, Arizona area. I was reluctant to commit all necessary funds from my personal bank account. However, by teaming up with my IRA, I was able to take advantage of that investment. I used some of my personal funds as well as some funds in my IRA. Before I could invest in real estate I had to roll the funds in my IRA (which was held by a traditional IRA administrator) out to a self-directed IRA. This investment generated double my money in a relatively short period of time. While such investment success is rare, it did reinforce my notion that investing in real estate is definitely a subject matter worth pursuing.

An investment in assets such as local real estate can give you a far greater sense of control than an investment in stock or mutual funds where the investments are typically in distant corporations. While this is admittedly a personal belief, I would be willing to bet that many of you agree.

DISADVANTAGES OF A SELF-DIRECTED IRA

Although I think the advantages of the self-directed IRA are compelling, there are some disadvantages which you need to at least be aware of:

- The fully self-directed IRA administrator's personnel are typically helpful in advising you of what you can and cannot do with the assets of your IRA. However, you cannot totally rely on the advice of such personnel and you can get yourself into trouble if you do not know the rules about what is allowable and what is not allowable with respect to IRA investments.

- An area that is particularly ripe for getting into trouble is where you set up a limited liability company and the limited liability company has control over its own checkbook in terms of expenditures. Often times this can result in prohibited transactions without anyone being aware of it. The reason a person uses a limited liability company is for flexibility in that the limited liability company can maintain a checking account so all expenses do not need to be run through the IRA administrator. Because of the potential for prohibited transaction as well as some additional paperwork needed when using an LLC, I would not recommend this to a neophyte. I will leave it up to the more experienced investors to decide whether to pursue this route or not.

- There are numerous pitfalls in the area of IRA and 401(k) investment in real estate, but I will endeavor in this book to tell you what is safe and where you need to seek further guidance.

The true self-directed IRA administrator does not provide you advice on your investments. For example, the IRA administrator will not tell you whether a building or a tract of undeveloped land which you are thinking about investing in is a good investment. Therefore, you must depend upon yourself or other experts you hire to make investment decisions for you, because the self-directed IRA administrator will not give you advice on possible investments.

WHAT IS A 401(K) PLAN?

Although 401(k) plans are discussed in more detail later, it seems wise to talk about them briefly at this point since 401(k) plans have become so popular and are such a significant part of the retirement landscape these days. This is particularly true with the ongoing demise of the traditional corporate pension plan.

The following bullet points summarize certain key aspects of the 401(k) plan:

- 401(k) plan is an employer-sponsored plan whereby the employee contributes funds to an account which will later be used for his or her retirement. Typically, the employer matches the employee's funds up to a certain amount to encourage the employee to make contributions to the retirement plan.

The following is a diagram that may be of help to you in visualizing in the 401(k) plan:

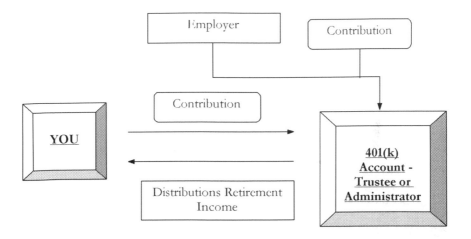

Again, it is important to remember that the 401(k) plan account maintained for you is separate from you.

- Also, it may be useful to think of a 401(k) plan as an umbrella. Under the general 401(k) plan adopted by the employer, the various employees have separate accounts. It is only the particular account to which the employee makes contributions which is referenced herein as the employee's 401(k) plan account. It is only from the value of this account that the employee will receive distributions in retirement. It is also only the particular account over which the employee has some control as to investments. The choice of investments is limited to those allowable under the employer's 401(k) plan generally.

- 401(k) plans are defined contribution plans. This means that certain amounts are contributed to the employee's account under the plan and the growth of the account is up to the investment choices by the employee within the range of options offered by the employer. Typically, the trustee or administrator is a bank, and the investment choices will be limited to a specified family of mutual funds.

- Unlike IRAs, these plans are subject to ERISA, the Employment Retirement Income Security Act of 1974. ERISA contains a number of rules. Plans subject to ERISA must follow these rules.

- Many of the concepts I will discuss related to IRAs also apply to 401(k)s, although 401(k)s are by their nature not so easy to self-direct. More on that later in this book.

- The 401(k) does provide certain advantages with regard to investments generating unrelated business taxable income.

While 401(k) funds as well as IRA funds can be invested in real estate, you may find that larger employers often resist any sort of changes to their existing 401(k) plan. However, there are a number of possibilities that may allow you to invest 401(k) funds in real estate even before you leave or change jobs.

Perhaps the easiest is to simply have a change of trustee to one that allows for investments in real estate. Another alternative is, with a cooperative employer, a termination of employment followed by a rehiring so that you have a break in service allowing for a distribution out to an IRA. There may also be opportunities for in-service distributions once you have reached certain ages, depending upon what your plan may provide.

Much easier is the case where you have funds from a 401(k) with a former employer. These can easily be moved into an IRA and the resulting IRA can be invested in real estate. Some of these rollovers from 401(k) plans can result in substantial IRAs.

I know some of this is awfully dry, but I thought it important that I cover some of this with you so that you have some idea of what IRAs and 401(k)s are all about before getting into the more interesting aspects of investment in real estate. Now on to these.

Next Chapter

In the next chapter we will focus on why IRAs are such a hot topic right now. If you will turn to the next chapter you may find an idea that you may want to pursue.

Chapter 2

Why Is This A Particularly Hot Topic Now?

Introduction

IRA investment in real estate is a particularly hot topic right now because the rules on converting traditional IRAs into Roth IRAs are changing. See the discussion below under "Converting Existing IRAs—Old Rules" and the further discussion at "New Rules on Conversion." Because of these changes in the rules, many people are focusing on IRAs right now.

A Primer on Roth IRAs

Recall that unlike a normal IRA, contributions to the Roth IRA are not deductible (contributions to a normal or traditional IRA are often deductible). However, the benefit to the Roth IRA is that unlike the traditional IRA, most withdrawals from the Roth are not taxable. Distributions or withdrawals from a normal or traditional IRA do result in taxable income to the recipient.

The earnings of both the normal or traditional IRA and the Roth IRA are generally tax free—subject to the rules on unrelated business taxable income. Another advantage of the Roth IRA is that you can make contributions to the Roth IRA after age 70½ when under the traditional IRA you would have had to start taking distributions by then and could no longer make contributions.

Depending upon your projected tax brackets in retirement as compared to your current tax brackets, the Roth IRA [or its 401(k) sibling, the Roth 401(k)] may be of interest to you. If you project that your tax brackets will be higher in retirement, whether because of changes in the tax law or otherwise, then the Roth may be very attractive to you. In addition, the Roth may be attractive to people who think their IRA is going to increase significantly in

9

value, so that taking out distributions in retirement will be considerably more costly even if you project your current tax brackets will remain the same or possibly even be somewhat reduced in retirement.

For example, let's say the Smiths are both currently employed and earning significant salaries. They also live in a state like North Carolina which has a fairly high personal income tax rate. Therefore, the combined tax brackets of the Smiths currently are high. They project that once they retire their tax brackets will drop from 36% down to less than 20%. They plan to move to Florida which has no state income tax. They also project that their IRA will not increase substantially in value between now and when they plan to retire.

The Roth IRA is not necessarily attractive to the Smiths. They project that their tax brackets in retirement will be lower than their tax brackets now, so the deductions for contributions to a traditional IRA are more valuable to them than the ability to take out tax free distributions in retirement. In addition, the Smiths need to take into account that the conversion of their existing IRA from a traditional IRA to a Roth IRA involves a current tax (divided over two years for conversions in 2010) on the value of the IRA.

Compare this to the Joneses. Mr. Jones is working but Mrs. Jones is a homemaker who does not have an income. They also live in South Carolina which has a lower personal income tax rate. Their combined tax bracket now is only 20%. They believe that this 20% bracket will actually go up in retirement because they believe there will be changes in the tax law which will increase tax rates. They also plan to continue to reside in South Carolina in retirement. They also believe that their IRAs will be invested in real estate and that the value of their IRAs will increase significantly in value between now and the time they retire. Given all this, the Roth IRA may be more attractive for them. This is because the current deductibility of contributions to the traditional IRA is not that valuable to them but the ability to take distributions out tax free in retirement is much more valuable. Moreover, the tax cost of converting a traditional to a Roth IRA would not be as expensive for them since they are currently in a lower tax bracket.

There is also the Roth 401(k) which works very much like the IRA but is subject to the 401(k) rules.

MORE ON THE DISTRIBUTIONS FROM A ROTH IRA

Unlike the normal or traditional IRA, the Roth IRA is not subject to the normal distribution rules so you do not have to begin taking distributions at age 70½. For this reason, the Roth IRA may be very attractive to persons who do not anticipate needing the income from their IRAs and instead want to pass the assets accumulated in their IRAs on to their heirs as an inheritance. This could make the Roth IRA very appealing to relatively wealthy people.

Keep in mind that while the income of an IRA is generally nontaxable (subject to the rules on unrelated taxable income) and the distributions from a Roth IRA are not taxable for income tax purposes, the IRA is nonetheless subject to estate tax.

Converting Existing IRAs—Old Rules

For years there have been provisions that allow for the conversion of a traditional IRA into a Roth IRA. However, this conversion could take place only if your adjusted gross income did not exceed $100,000 (other than married individuals filing separately). These rules effectively eliminated the conversion of a traditional or normal IRA into a Roth IRA for all taxpayers with significant incomes.

New Rules on Conversion

The rules however have changed and beginning in 2010 you can convert your traditional IRA into a Roth IRA irrespective of your income level. This change is permanent so you can take advantage of the conversion opportunity at any time. One note: there is a tax savings if you do the conversion in 2010. More on that below.

Beware of the price tag. Upon the conversion of a traditional into a Roth IRA the value of the IRA on the date of conversion is treated as taxable income. If you convert in 2010 then, absent an election to the contrary, no portion of the gross income from the conversion is included in income for 2010 but rather one-half of the income resulting from the conversion is included in gross income for 2011 and the other half in 2012. While higher income taxpayers can still convert their regular IRAs into Roth IRAs after 2010, this additional tax break of being able to spread out the tax liability resulting from the conversion is limited to conversions accomplished in 2010. Whether you take advantage of this tax break depends on where you believe rates are headed. If you believe rates are headed up, you may elect to go ahead and pay the tax on the conversion currently in 2010 rather than spreading out the income into 2011 and 2012.

While the conversion is not for everyone, it is certainly something to consider and something that has caused interest in IRAs generally and IRA investment in real estate specifically to be on the increase. If you think the value of a real estate investment that you are making through your IRA will increase substantially in value then the Roth IRA may be attractive to you.

What if I Change My Mind?

If you convert your traditional IRA into a Roth IRA and decide later that you made a mistake, you will have until October 15th of the year after making the Roth conversion to reverse the process.

Another Example of Why You Might Want to Convert

Let's say that your IRA is buying an apartment building and you project that you will have 22 years before your retirement and a further 30 years after that of life expectancy. You further project that the apartment building which is worth $50,000 today will be worth $150,000 when you retire and $300,000 when you ultimately die.

This may be a case where you are willing to convert in 2010 and pay the tax on the current value of the apartment building over two years. Since you are dealing with a recent purchase the current value is likely to be the purchase price.

You could then take a distribution of the apartment building tax free at retirement. If you do not think you will need the apartment building, then you might want to convert to the Roth IRA, take distributions equal to the rent net of expenses and then pass the IRA containing the apartment building on to your heirs. Again, remember that while the distributions from a Roth IRA are not subject to income tax, the Roth IRA will be subject to estate tax when it passes on to your heirs.

Therefore, when you die, if you pass your IRA on to your children then the IRA will be subject to a layer of tax in the form of the federal estate tax. This assumes, of course, that there is any federal estate tax in effect. Currently there is no estate tax for 2010 but then the estate tax comes back with the million dollar exemption in 2011. Commentators keep saying that Congress must deal with this situation but, to date, they have not.

Therefore, assuming there is a federal estate tax, the $300,000 value of the apartment building at your death will be included in your estate for federal estate tax purposes.

Next Chapter

In the next chapter you will learn what investments are allowable in an IRA and whether IRA investment in real estate is something new. The knowledge of what investments are allowable in an IRA should be of great value to you.

CHAPTER 3

Is IRA Investment in Real Estate Something New?

INTRODUCTION

There is nothing new about the notion of an IRA investing in real estate. Essentially, we have been able to invest in real estate ever since IRAs came into existence, but in my experience the usual banks and brokerage firms that are holding IRAs do not push this form of investment.

Different firms may have their reasons for not advocating IRA investment in real estate, but one common reason is that the investment in real estate involves more paperwork and is more complicated and slightly more expensive than investment in the normal stock and bond based mutual funds offered by banks and brokerage firms. Your bank or brokerage firm may quite possibly have not even told you about real estate as an investment option for your IRA. Moreover, the investment is not restricted to IRAs but is available to other types of plans such as 401(k)s.

You'll recall the 401(k) is another type of employee retirement plan that allows for employee contributions which are often matched by the employer. As with the IRA, the employee generally has some choices as to the type of investment. The choices are usually based on whoever is handling the 401(k) plan and are typically limited to a handful of mutual funds.

Like the IRA, investment in real estate by a 401(k) is perfectly legal but it is often times impractical because the administrator of the 401(k) plan is not willing to allow for investment in real estate. One obvious solution to this is to change administrators or to move the 401(k) plan to an administrator which does allow for investment in real estate. This will, of course, require some action by the employer. You likely will need to push the employer to make this happen. Also, the more employees who raise this issue with the employer, the more likely it is the employer will move the 401(k) plan to a different administrator.

WHAT CAN MY IRA OR OTHER PLAN INVEST IN?

Given the ups and downs of the stock market and a growing concern among people about whether they will have enough to retire on comfortably, the question naturally arises as to what a person's 401(k), IRA, or other plan can be invested in. The question is particularly pertinent because so many of us have such a large portion of our savings in IRAs and qualified plans of one sort or another. 401(k)s in particular are a very prevalent form of qualified plan.

The way the rules are laid out, the real question is not what can my IRA invest in but rather what can my IRA not invest in? I say this because the answer is that your IRA or qualified plan can invest in anything with three exceptions:

1. A life insurance policy on the life of the IRA owner.
2. Collectibles, with certain exceptions.
3. Subchapter S corporation stock. (This is not really a prohibition, but as discussed below, this is not something you want to do.)

Each of these three items is discussed more specifically below, but before getting into these briefly, I will focus on what this book is really all about which is investment in real estate.

CAN I INVEST IN REAL ESTATE?

Absolutely! If you read the discussion below and the list above, you will see that real estate is not on the list of the three things you cannot invest in.

Your IRA can not only invest directly in various types of real estate, but also in debt obligations secured by real estate or in entities (such as a limited liability company) investing in real estate. The only caution here is that you need to be aware of the prohibited transaction rules and the taxability of unrelated debt financed income which are both discussed later in this book. Moreover, you can not only invest in real estate in its various forms but also in different assets related to real estate.

The following is a list of just some possible investments that you can make through your IRA:

*   Undeveloped land

*   Leases

*   Interests in limited liability companies

*   Interests in limited partnerships

14

- Interests in corporations (although there may be some tax reasons for not wanting to invest in a corporation holding real estate)
- Single family homes (although these cannot be used as your personal residence until a distribution is made from your IRA). You can invest in a house through your IRA and either resell it at a profit or rent it. There are restrictions on your ability to do any work on the house yourself which we will touch on briefly below.
- Multi-family rental property
- Other types of rental property
- Strip shopping centers
- Office buildings
- Foreign real estate
- Tax certificates
- Notes and deeds of trust.

This list is by no means exclusive, but gives you some idea of the types of investments that you can make beyond the typical stocks and bonds and mutual funds which are always available through self-directed IRAs as well as the more traditional IRAs. Essentially, all IRAs are to some extent self-directed in that you can designate the types of investments that your IRA will hold. However, many banks and brokerage firms limit you to just the mutual funds they typically offer together with whatever investment products they offer. The true self-directed IRA allows you to invest in anything which is legal. Therefore, if you move to a fully self-directed IRA, you can still invest in stocks and bonds but also have available the option of investing in real estate and any other legal investment.

Remember that even though the investment in real estate is perfectly legal, you will also find that many existing Trustees of IRAs and 401(k)s do not want to deal with investments in real estate, so you may end up having to make a move to one which allows for self-directed investments in assets such as real estate and other nontraditional assets. There are a number of custodians which are willing to allow you to invest your IRA or 401(k) on a self-directed basis. Two of the prominent ones I am personally familiar with are Entrust New Direction IRA and Pensco.

There are counterparts to the self-directed IRA in the form of 401(k) plans that allow for self-direction.

Why Have I not Heard About This?

Most of the traditional trustees and custodians of IRAs and other qualified plans are banks, brokerage firms and similar institutions which do not traditionally focus on real estate investments. It has always been easier for them to recommend stock, bond and mutual fund investments rather than dealing with real estate investments.

Having to handle the necessary paperwork to allow for real estate investments is simply less profitable for the custodians and trustees so they tend to stay away from talking to you about those possible investments. In their defense, why would any IRA trustee or custodian want to help you select assets which are more trouble and less profitable for them to invest your IRA funds in?

Why Should the Average person Care?

There are a number of forces from the drop in the stock market to the need to provide for your own retirement that are driving people to look at real estate as a possible investment. Given that investment in real estate is perfectly legal and permissible for your IRA, you should take away from this chapter at least the thought that it is worth your effort to learn more about investments in real estate by your IRA or 401(k).

Why Should Syndicators or Other Professionals Care?

There are tremendous opportunities to purchase real estate in the current market. Given these opportunities and the fact that syndicators and other real estate professionals may not have sufficient funds of their own to pursue the many opportunities available, such professionals are on the lookout for sources of capital that can be tapped to allow such purchases. The money locked within IRAs and other qualified plans is immense and is an ideal source of such capital for investment in real estate.

For the reputable syndicator and other real estate professional, this can be a win-win situation. The syndicator or other professional can profit from the investment in real estate while providing a solid return to the IRAs or 401(k) s investing with the real estate professional.

Many IRA owners, once exposed to the concept of investment in real estate, find the idea appealing. However, they are not necessarily equipped to make the best decisions in terms of investments. Syndicators and other real estate professionals can provide them options for real estate investment while the syndicator or other real estate professional also receives a return or fee for their services.

What Can My IRA not Invest In? —Revisited

Earlier there was a listing of three things that IRAs cannot or should not invest in. Each of these is dealt with in greater detail below.

What Is the Limitation on Investment in Life Insurance?

The Internal Revenue Code (the "Code") specifically requires that the written governing instrument creating an IRA must provide that no part of the IRAs funds will be invested in life insurance contracts. The Code also deals specifically with investment in endowment contracts and provides that any life insurance element in an endowment contract is to be treated as distributed to the IRA owner.

While the prohibition on investments in life insurance does not carry over to qualified plans, often times the plan documents offered by the various available trustees or custodians will not allow for investment in life insurance or will allow for only limited investment in life insurance. Moreover, the content of the prototype plan documents must be approved by the IRS, so, as a practical matter, you may be restricted on investment in life insurance in qualified plans as well.

You will need to check your plan documents or consult with your trustee or custodian if you are really interested in having your IRA or other retirement plan invest in an insurance policy on your life.

I would suggest that you simply assume that your IRA or other qualified plan may not invest in life insurance policies on your life and look at other allowable investments instead.

What Are Collectibles and What Are the Consequences of Investing in Them?

Generally, investments in collectibles are penalized. The following are examples of collectibles:

- works of art

- rugs

- antiques

- metals (except as provided below with respect to certain coins)

- gems

- stamps

- alcoholic beverages (e.g., vintage wines)

- musical instruments

- historical objects (such as documents or clothes)

- most coins (with the exception noted below)
- other items of tangible personal property that the IRS determines are collectibles

There is an exception allowing investments in one, one-half, one-quarter, or one-tenth ounce U.S. gold coins or one ounce silver coins minted by the Treasury Department as well as certain platinum coins and certain gold, silver, palladium, and platinum bullion.

The impact of investing in a collectible is that the investment is regarded as being distributed to the IRA owner at its fair market value in the year of the investment and as if the distribution was made in the year of purchase. This can mean ordinary income arises in an amount equal to the fair market value. In addition, if the IRA owner is under age 59½, the "deemed distribution" is subject to a 10% additional tax based on the value of the collectibles.

In other words, this is not something you want to have happen.

The same penalty for investments in collectibles does carry over into the qualified plan area.

The reason for this rule is that, early on, professionals such as doctors and others were investing their IRAs in works of art and other collectibles. The IRS wanted to put a stop to this and therefore imposed these rules, making investment in collectibles cost prohibitive for most people.

WHAT IS THE ISSUE ON INVESTMENT IN SUBCHAPTER S CORPORATION STOCK?

There is not actually a prohibition against your IRA investing in the stock of a Subchapter S corporation, but if you do invest the IRA in a Subchapter S corporation, the corporation will be disqualified under Subchapter S and will become a taxable corporation under Subchapter C. This is because only certain types of trusts can qualify to own Subchapter S corporation stock without terminating the Subchapter S election. An IRA does not qualify as an allowable trust.

In other words, you do not want to invest in the stock of a Subchapter S corporation because the investment will eliminate the favorable tax treatment afforded the Subchapter S corporation. While this may not impact you, particularly if the only stock in the corporation you hold is through your IRA which is generally exempt from income tax (with the exception of unrelated business taxable income as discussed later), the other stockholders are likely to be very unhappy if your IRA's investment terminates the qualification for Subchapter S status for all of them.

You might ask why the Subchapter S classification is so attractive. The short answer is that a Subchapter S corporation is taxed generally like a partnership. 'What this means is that rather than the income (or loss) being taxed to the corporation, it is passed through and picked up on the stockholders' personal returns. Also, distributions of cash are not generally regarded as dividends. A full discussion of Subchapter S corporations could take up a whole book in itself, but this should be enough to .explain to you why the Subchapter S classification is very valuable to those who have made a Subchapter S election.

However, effective for taxable years beginning after 1997, Code §401 qualified plan trusts are eligible to hold Subchapter S corporation stock, so your 401(k) will be allowed to invest in the stock of a Subchapter S corporation without disqualifying the corporation as a Subchapter S corporation for federal income tax purposes. However, in my experience, most administrators of 401(k) plans are not interested in allowing you to invest in the stock of Subchapter S corporations which tend to be closely held corporations, meaning that they are held by a very limited number of stockholders. Therefore, this ability to invest in Subchapter S corporation stock is more theoretical than a real advantage of 401(k)s.

Next Chapter

The next chapter will focus on why you should care that real estate is an allowable investment for your IRA or 401(k) plan account. Your financial future may depend on this information.

CHAPTER 4

Why Should the Average Person Be Interested in Investment by IRAs in Real Estate?

INTRODUCTION

The average person should be interested in the investment options available to their IRAs or qualified plans generally, and the allowability of investments in real estate specifically, for a number of reasons.

The first is the uncertainty regarding the stock market and the loss of wealth which has occurred in the stock market. Even though the worst of the stock market drop appears to be over, at least for now, the stock market continues to experience significant volatility. There always seems to be a new worry affecting the market. If it is not the financial problems of the United States, then it is concern over the debt of Greece and other European countries. Significant on-going volatility seems to have become the rule rather than the exception.

Secondly, there is a growing realization that you need to take care of your own retirement rather than depend upon the government or your employer to provide for your retirement. People are beginning to realize that retirement plans they may have counted on may not be available or, if available, will not provide the sort of incomes they had hoped for.

Given these factors, the owner of an IRA, 401(k) or other qualified plan should be interested in the possibilities offered by investment in real estate. While investment in real estate may not be for everyone, it is clearly an alternative that must be considered by any person serious about their retirement. Your financial future may hinge on the decisions you make with respect to the investments in your IRA or 401(k) plan account. The IRA or 401(k) plan account is for many people their largest source of capital.

Before touching on some of the reasons that you might be concerned about your retirement, I will focus first on investments in real estate which is what this book is really all about.

INVESTMENT IN REAL ESTATE

While you should not look at any investment in real estate as being the sole answer to your retirement needs, it is something for you to at least consider. At the very least, an investment in real estate provides further diversification for the assets of your IRA or 401(k).

Moreover, while some investments in real estate can be regarded as speculative and there is no guarantee that any investment in real estate will not result in a loss (just as there are no guarantees on other investments), many real estate investments can provide you with significant returns as well. Those who maintained their investments in the stock market through the recent decline can attest to the fact that an investment in stocks is certainly not without risk.

Because of the significant erosion in wealth coming out of the drop in the stock market coupled with the elimination or reduction of the traditional pension plan and the uncertainty surrounding social security, some people feel the need to take chances with their investments to make up for the decline. An investment in real estate may offer this opportunity.

This is particularly true now because the crash in the United States economy not only influenced the stock market but also reduced real estate prices substantially. The lack of lending has further reduced the prices of real estate. During any time period when prices are depressed, those who are able to buy assets can look forward to a favorable return on those investments.

Moreover, investment in real estate as opposed to the stock market provides an additional advantage in that a particular real estate asset is more personal in the sense that a particular real estate asset can be viewed and followed by the layman. Moreover, the fortunes of a particular real estate investment in a particular area arguably can be followed more closely than can be the fortunes of a mutual fund investing in the stocks of a number of distant companies. While strictly an intangible benefit, there is something comforting about driving by a piece of real estate, whether raw land or developed, and knowing that you own that real estate or some interest in it.

EXAMPLE OF WHY INVESTMENT IN REAL ESTATE CAN BE ATTRACTIVE

Let us turn for a second to Mary who has found an apartment building which she is purchasing through her IRA. After paying various expenses, including a mortgage, the IRA is left with $2,000 per month which it can distribute out to Mary. Do you feel an extra $2,000 per month might make your retirement a little more comfortable? For most of us, the answer would be a resounding yes. The question, of course, is how much money it takes to buy the apartment building and what you are giving up in terms of other returns on that money.

Reasons Why the Average person Might Want to Look at an Investment in Real Estate

Some of these reasons have been touched on before, but basically there are a number of reasons why the average person might want to consider an investment in real estate because of occurrences outside of real estate. These reasons are discussed further below.

The Stock Market

Many of you have experienced the substantial drops in the stock market over the past few years. If you have had the nerve to look at your IRA or 401(k) statements, assuming that your IRA or 401(k) is invested directly in the stock market or indirectly in mutual funds investing in stocks, then you have experienced first hand the feeling in the pit of your stomach seeing your investments drop precipitously and possibly your retirement plans with them. The newspapers have been full of information regarding the evaporation of personal wealth because of the stock market drop. Moreover, many of you have probably experienced the need to put your retirement plans on hold until better days.

Because of the substantial drops in the stock market, many people have sworn off investment in the stock market both directly and through their IRAs or qualified plans. Moreover, some experts are now questioning whether investments in the stock market are the way to go in planning for retirement. Although the market is in the process of some semblance of recovery now, there obviously are no guarantees for the future. Moreover, there is a significant degree of volatility in the market and future prospects for the market are anything but clear.

Many people are concerned about the direction of this country and the degree of government interference in the capital markets. Many others are concerned about the significant deficits facing this country and the possibility of significant inflationary trends in the future.

Moreover, even if you are not at the point of giving up on the stock market, many investment advisers indicate that the key to a sound investment plan is diversification. Investment in real estate certainly provides an additional form of diversification.

THE ELIMINATION OF THE PENSION PLAN

In addition to this evaporation of personal wealth in the form of investment in the stock market, many if not most companies are cutting out the traditional pension plan that so many people had counted on to provide their retirement. These people are increasingly realizing that they need to look to their own savings and their IRAs and 401(k)s and other qualified plans to provide them a retirement.

Moreover, even where a pension plan is in place, the amount paid is often times limited and there are no guarantees that the pension will be available for people retiring in the future.

The days of working for a single employer who would provide a comfortable retirement to you are largely a thing of the past. We have seen in the past few years the failures of major companies and most which have survived are looking for ways to reduce their obligations. The liabilities represented by pension plans are significant and many companies are looking critically at the desirability of maintaining their pension funds in the future.

INABILITY TO COUNT ON SOCIAL SECURITY

We also all know about the financial issues involved in the social security system in particular and the United States government in general. We are already running record deficits in this country and there appears no end in sight to this. All one has to do is look at the business pages in the local newspaper or watch the news on any given day to see how large of a deficit we are facing in this country and the debts that will have to be dealt with at some point, either through increased taxes or reduced benefits or both.

While you may be able to count on social security for now, there are no guarantees it will be available forever. Between the fact the baby boomers are reaching retirement age and the overall joblessness level in this country, a record number of persons were added to the social security system last year.

It certainly does not seem to make sense to plan on social security as the cornerstone of your retirement. While I am not suggesting that you ignore the benefits available through social security, you may want to consider these benefits, as I do, as icing on the retirement cake. I do think it makes sense to plan on having a sufficient amount in retirement if social security should be unavailable or reduced. You should have a plan in place for what you would do if social security were unavailable or significantly reduced.

NEXT CHAPTER

Now that you are convinced that your financial future may depend upon the investment choices with respect to the assets in your IRA or qualified plan, the next chapter will focus on the particular concerns of syndicators, brokers, real estate agents and other real estate professionals. If you are not one of these people you may nonetheless just want to skim over the chapter because there is some useful information in there for you as well. Moreover, even if you are not concerned with the particular concerns of real estate professionals, the next chapter contains a very helpful question and answer series that summarizes much of what is allowable and not allowable with respect to IRA investment in real estate.

CHAPTER 5

Why Should Syndicators, Brokers, Real Estate Agents and Other Real Estate Professionals Be Interested in IRA Investment in Real Estate?

OPPORTUNITY AND RESPONSIBILITY INTERSECT

For syndicators as well as real estate agents, brokers and other real estate professionals already working in the real estate business, there are opportunities as well as pitfalls in assisting clients who wish to invest their IRA funds in real estate.

Syndicators are looking for sources of capital given the many opportunities in the real estate market. There has already been a well-publicized downturn in the housing market and the commercial real estate market. All of this is serving to drive down prices.

There's a large amount of capital currently in IRAs and other retirement plans to access that capital, the syndicator needs to be aware of the rules applicable to IRAs and investment in real estate. As will be discussed a number of times throughout this book, the fact that the syndicator may form an LLC (short for a "limited liability company") in which IRAs will invest and it is the LLC that will invest in real estate, does not change the applicability of the rules. The syndicator must be well versed in the rules applicable to IRA investment or he will end up committing a prohibited transaction within the LLC. Not only will the syndicator potentially be in trouble for having committed the prohibited transaction, but he likely will have jeopardized the qualification of his investor's IRAs which obviously will make the investor most unhappy.

Brokers and real estate agents are surely going to be asked about IRA

27

investment in real estate and you cannot fulfill your responsibilities to your clients without having some knowledge of what is and what is not allowable. I cannot tell you how many times I have been asked about using an IRA to invest in the beach house. (This subject is dealt with in greater detail later in this chapter since it is a topic of such interest.)

Perhaps just as importantly, there are significant opportunities in that there is a great deal of capital in IRAs and the investment of this capital can result in commissions to the real estate broker or Realtor who takes the time to understand the rules regarding IRA investment in real estate.

PERIOD OF RETHINKING

Opportunities are waiting for you, particularly among baby boomers who are at or approaching retirement age. This group is giving more consideration to investments that will allow them to have a comfortable retirement. Beyond that, the volatility in the stock market has caused many investors to rethink their investment strategies as far as retirement goes. Such a period of rethinking investment strategies is an opportunity for syndicators, brokers and other professionals to present real estate as an alternative to stocks or mutual funds. Investment from IRAs in real estate can result in commissions to the real estate broker or real estate agent who takes the time to understand the rules.

MORE ON CAPITAL PRESENTLY AVAILABLE IN IRAS

IRAs represent a significant source of investment capital. In mid-2009 there was about $4 trillion in IRAs.

The amount of assets in IRAs has doubtless grown as further contributions are made to the various types of qualified plans. On top of the normal contributions, as the baby boomers reach certain ages they may make increased "make up" contributions intended to allow for those nearing retirement to increase their retirement funds in the years immediately prior to retirement.

An even greater source of the growth of IRA assets are rollovers from employer 401(k)s. Under the tax rules, when an employee leaves the employ of an employer which has a 401(k) plan, the former employee has the option of rolling the assets in his 401(k) account out to an IRA and, by doing so, deferring the tax on the amount in the account.

The amount of capital in IRAs is likely now growing as the unemployment rate has gone up and workers whose jobs have been eliminated have the option of rolling their 401(k)s from their former companies into IRAs. Moreover, as those who have retained their jobs decide to retire, then they will also have the same option of rolling over the significant amount of funds in company 401(k) plans they have accumulated into IRAs. If these assets are rolled into self-directed IRAs, then these funds will be available for investment in real estate.

Given the assets already in IRAs, the need for baby boomers to invest more as they near retirement, and the trend of former employees having the ability to roll their 401(k) funds into IRAs, IRAs represent a considerable and growing source of investment capital that the savvy syndicator, broker or other real estate professional should not ignore.

QUESTIONS AND ANSWERS

As indicated a number of times above, the syndicator or broker or Realtor or other real estate professional cannot take advantage of the opportunities provided by the funds in IRAs while still competently representing their investors and clients without a working knowledge of the rules which apply to investment in real estate by IRAs.

Perhaps the best way to get started with developing at least a basic understanding of what you can and cannot do with an IRA is by working through a series of questions and answers. Where I say something cannot be done, this often involves a prohibited transaction.

1. Can I sell real estate I already own to my own IRA?
    No; this would be a prohibited transaction.

2. Can my IRA purchase property from someone else?
    Yes; so long as it truly is a third party who is not related to you. You could not have your IRA purchase assets from certain family members such as your parents, your spouse, your children, grandchildren and other descendents and their spouses. However, there are exceptions having to do with related people and you could for example have your IRA purchase property from a brother or sister (and presumably their spouses).

    You also could not purchase property in your IRA from a company in which you or any of the prohibited related people own a 50% or greater interest.

    If the person or company is truly unrelated to you then your IRA can purchase property from he, she or it.

3. Can I sell property from my IRA to a family member?
    Maybe; you could sell property owned by your IRA to your brother or sister and their spouses. You cannot sell to the list of prohibited related people such as your parents, your spouse, your children and grandchildren and other descendents and their spouses Read on for more on this subject.

29

You also could not sell property to a company in which you or one of the prohibited related parties owns 50% or more.

4. Can I take a commission on a purchase by my IRA?

    I would say no; this would be a prohibited transaction. You would be profiting personally from a transaction in which your IRA was involved. The answer could be different regarding a client's IRA as discussed further below.

5. Can I take a commission on a sale of property by my IRA?

    No; this would be a prohibited transaction because you would be personally benefitting from a transaction in which your IRA was involved.

6. Can I receive a commission on a sale of property to someone else's IRA?

    Yes; so long as it is not the IRA of a family member (again a brother or a sister's IRA likely would be okay) or other prohibited person.

    This should be a prime area of additional business for brokers and real estate agents. As part of your conversations with your clients, you should talk to them about the possibility of purchasing additional properties in their IRAs. Each client who buys a house could potentially be a client for purchasing some other sort of real property in their IRA and you can receive commissions on these transactions.

7. What if my IRA purchases a foreclosed property that needs some fix-up? Can I do the work?

    No; you providing the work would be regarded as an additional contribution to your IRA in a form other than cash and also likely would result in your exceeding your contribution limits Allowable contributions to your IRA must be in cash, so you could not perform the work personally even if you were allowed to make a contribution to your IRA.

8. Can I manage property purchased by my IRA?

    Yes; at least in a limited sense. You could certainly collect rent checks as long as they are made payable to your IRA and you remit them immediately to your IRA administrator.

    You could also determine who should be hired to perform work on the property so long as all of the bills are paid by the administrator of your IRA out of funds held in your IRA. You cannot pay the bill as yourself from your personal funds, because this would likely involve impermissible excess contribution to your IRA.

9. Can I receive compensation for managing a property held in my IRA?

The answer to this is unclear. Even the IRA commentators seem split on this issue so you would be better off not taking the compensation.

10. Can I receive compensation for managing the property owned by the IRAs of others?

Yes; so long as the IRA is not owned by one of the prohibited related persons or entities.

This should again be a prime source of possible additional business for brokers and real estate agents if their clients begin using their IRAs to purchase properties. Keep in mind though that once you provide services to the plan you are arguably a disqualified person, so you should not later purchase property from the IRA.

11. Can my IRA lease property it owns to others?

Yes; again, you cannot lease property to one of the prohibited related parties such as yourself, your parents, your spouse, your children, their decedents and their spouses and companies in which you, together with any of these people, own 50% or more in interest.

However, you could lease property to your brother or sister and you certainly can lease property to an unrelated third party.

12. Can I receive a commission for leasing property owned by my IRA?

I believe the answer here is no that this would be a prohibited transaction.

13. Can I receive a commission for leasing property owned by the IRAs of others?

Yes; so long as the IRA is not owned by one of the prohibited related parties or a company owned 50% or more in interest by you and the prohibited related parties.

Again, this should be a prime source of potential additional business for brokers and real estate agents in that every client of yours who makes a purchase through their IRA may need assistance in leasing the property once their IRA owns it.

14. If I want to purchase a property with my IRA but my IRA does not have enough money, can I seek a loan to my IRA?

Yes; so long as the loan is non-recourse meaning the lender's only recourse is to the property itself. You cannot guarantee the loan. Seller financing is perfectly permissible. A loan guaranteed by an unrelated third party is also a possibility. The subject of using debt in connection with purchases by an IRA is discussed in more detail below.

15. What if the property is too expensive for my client's IRA?

    The loan route is obviously available to the client so long as the client does not guarantee the loan.

    In addition, a number of clients can pool their IRAs or their personal money to purchase a more expensive property either directly with each of them owning a percentage interest in the property or by formation of a limited liability company or other entity. In this case, the limited liability company or other entity would own the property and the IRAs and/or the clients with their personal money would own interests in the limited liability company or other entity.

    There may also be possibilities for you to team up with your IRA as long as you do not obtain a loan personally secured by property owned by your IRA. If you can secure a loan secured by property outside your IRA you could then team up with your IRA with both you and the IRA providing cash to purchase the property.

    You should be cautious of involving your own IRA if you wish to provide services to the client and receive compensation.

16. Can I use my IRA to secure a loan?

    No; not if you are trying to pledge your IRA assets to secure a loan personally.

17. Can I buy a vacation home in my IRA?

    *You are certainly going to be asked the question by potential clients if you mention that they can invest their IRAs in real estate. **The answer to this is yes even though the clients cannot use it themselves and also the home cannot** IRA and 401(k) Investment in Real Estate **be used by any of the prohibited related parties.***

18. What if I want to lease the vacation home to myself?

    Sorry; you cannot even lease the vacation home owned by your IRA to yourself or one of the prohibited related parties.

19. Is there any legal way to acquire the vacation home?

    Sure; your IRA can clearly acquire the vacation home so long as you do not use it (at least until you take it as a distribution from your IRA) and other prohibited people do not use it. Your IRA could clearly purchase the home intended to be a vacation home in the future and lease it to unrelated parties. If you ever wanted to use the vacation home yourself, you could take a distribution of the home from your IRA and pay tax on the distribution.

Let's say that you are a Realtor and that for each person you sell a house to you are also able to help them invest their IRA in some sort of commercial property and you receive a commission for that. Would you be interested in an extra few thousand dollars a month? If the answer to this is yes, then you need to understand what is and is not allowable for IRA and other qualified plan investments in real estate.

CONCLUSION

As should be obvious from the questions and answers above, there is significant opportunity for the broker, Realtor or syndicator who is willing to devote some time to understanding the rules related to investment in real estate by an IRA or 401(k). Most obviously, there are commissions to be earned from transactions by IRAs and 401(k) plans which represent a sizeable pool of investment capital which should not be ignored. Syndicators should be very interested in the pool of capital held by IRAs and 401(k)s as a source of capital for investments in the real estate market.

All that is required to work in this area is to put some time and effort into understanding the rules that are applied to IRAs. Portions of this book will further flesh out the concepts touched on in the questions and answers above. Give yourself a competitive advantage, and read on to learn more.

NEXT CHAPTER

The next chapter will teach you about straightforward investments in real estate. These are the sort of investments that should be safe for you to pursue without being unduly complex.

CHAPTER 6

Straightforward Investments in Real Estate

WHAT DO I MEAN BY A STRAIGHTFORWARD INVESTMENT IN REAL ESTATE?

While there is a risk inherent to any investment, there are three key elements to what I would describe as a straightforward or relatively safe real estate investment by an IRA (discounting of course the risk inherent in any investment).

The first is an IRA that allows for investments in real estate. Typically, this would require a self-directed IRA with a custodian or trustee that would allow for investment in real estate.

The second is that the purchase be from an allowable person who would typically be a stranger or other nondisqualified person. The subject of who is a disqualified person is dealt with in greater detail later.

Third, the IRA has to have sufficient cash to allow for the purchase of the real estate as well as any anticipated expenses in excess of income. It is also prudent to have a reserve for unexpected expenses.

Each of these three elements is discussed in greater detail in turn below.

OPENING A SELF-DIRECTED IRA

If your IRA trustee or custodian allows for an investment in real estate, the next questions become locating a suitable real estate investment and then determining what sort of paperwork the trustee or custodian requires for it.

If your current trustee doesn't allow real estate investments, you or the owner of the IRA may need to roll the funds from the current IRA into one offered by a trustee or custodian that allows for self-directed investments in real estate.

Each custodian or administrator that allows for self-directed IRAs will have its own paperwork as far as setting up the account. Normally, there will be some sort of an application and a fee disclosure statement.

You will also have to determine how to initially fund the IRA whether it be a cash contribution, a rollover from an existing IRA or a rollover from your account under an employer's 401(k) plan. The administrator for the new IRA can provide you with the necessary paperwork to open the IRA.

With that done then you are ready for self-directed investments in real estate. The next steps in this process are determining what paperwork the self-directed IRA administrator will need in order to invest your IRA funds in a particular real estate asset and then determining who you can deal with.

Paperwork for A Particular Real Estate Investment

Each IRA administrator will also have paperwork that must be completed in connection with your IRA's acquisition of a particular real estate asset. For example, you may be asked to complete and execute a buy direction form so that the IRA administrator knows where to send funds from your IRA and has your direction that this is an investment that has been made for your IRA.

The investment should be made in the name of the IRA administrator on behalf of your IRA. For example, Pam has decided to purchase an apartment building in her IRA. She has her deed for the apartment building made out in the name of her IRA administrator as administrator of her IRA. She would have the deed made out to Entrust as administrator of Pam's IRA so the deed would read "Entrust New Direction IRA fbo Pam Jones."

To avoid potential problems it is best to begin the process with the contract in the name of the IRA administrator.

Purchase from Permitted Individuals

The second key element is that the purchase be from an allowable person.

If the property is purchased from someone totally unrelated to the IRA owner, is not purchased from an entity in which the IRA owner has a significant ownership interest and is purchased from someone not in any way involved in providing services to the IRA, then the purchase should qualify as allowable. Purchases from strangers are clearly allowed.

However, purchases from certain persons, including the IRA owner himself or herself, will result in a prohibited transaction. Therefore, the IRA owner cannot transfer property he or she already owns to his or her IRA.

Also, you could not purchase property in your IRA from your parents or children.

There is a large universe of people who are not disqualified persons. It is perfectly permissible for your IRA to purchase property from such non-disqualified persons. Anytime you are purchasing property from true third parties who are not in any way related to you or involved with your IRA, you should be safe.

SUFFICIENT CASH FOR PURCHASE AND MAINTENANCE

The third element of a straightforward or relatively safe investment in real estate is that the IRA contains sufficient cash not only to provide the purchase price but also to provide for any expenses in excess of the rental income anticipated from the purchased property. Keep in mind that the IRA must pay for all expenses and upkeep such as insurance, utilities, taxes and the like to the extent these are not paid by the tenant. Also, the IRA, like any property owner, will be responsible for necessary capital expenditures such as roof replacement and HVAC (heating and air conditioning) repairs and replacement, etc.

For a commercial property the expense of maintaining a parking lot and exterior lighting may also be significant and again must be paid for out of funds in the IRA, unless the property is leased to a tenant under what is often referred to as a triple net lease. Under such a so-called net lease, the tenant is responsible for many of the expenses of the upkeep of the property, including insurance premiums and taxes.

However, even in the typical triple net lease, the landlord is still responsible for certain capital items such as roof and parking lot expenses. If you purchase a property subject to a lease, my best advice is to carefully examine the lease and determine what expenses are the responsibility of the tenant and what expenses are the responsibility of the landlord, which in this case is your IRA or 401(k) plan account.

Also, keep in mind that the IRA owner cannot provide sweat equity such as painting the beach house. Not only would this involve a non-cash contribution to the IRA but their efforts likely would be regarded as an excess contribution to their IRA. This means that as a practical matter, the IRA must have sufficient funds to take care of such things as painting and the like, and the IRA owner cannot count on providing these services.

In addition to having sufficient cash for all of the projected expenses of maintaining the property, the IRA or 401(k) plan account also should have a reserve against unexpected items. Examples of unexpected items could be damage from a storm or other natural disaster or by human beings in the form of looting or vandalism. One thing that being involved in real estate has taught me is that it is difficult to anticipate all of the possible expenses that may arise in a particular case.

In the most straightforward and safest real estate transaction, this means the IRA must contain sufficient funds to do all of these things. The IRA owner can also take into account anticipated contributions to the IRA in calculating the cash available. Moreover, in the straightforward real estate investment, no debt is needed and no funds are needed from other parties to accomplish the purchase and upkeep of the real estate.

Turning back to Pam again, the apartment building she plans on buying will cost her IRA $600,000 and the total annual rent she anticipates the IRA will receive is $100,000. Out of this $100,000 her IRA is to pay $50,000 in mortgage payments, $5,000 in property taxes, and $5,000 in insurance. She also sets aside $10,000 a year to cover capital items such as roof replacement, parking lot repair and/or replacement and HVAC system replacement. She should also set aside some amount for unexpected expenditures such as $5,000 and can only count on her IRA receiving the net of $25,000. Also because Pam's IRA secured a mortgage, her IRA may be liable for some unrelated business tax which would further reduce the $25,000 the IRA expects to net. If the apartment goes up in value then Pam's IRA can sell it somewhere down the road and hopefully generate a profit (again, unrelated business taxable income may be due if the mortgage has not been paid off in advance of the sale).

What to Do in the Case of an Unexpected Shortfall

It seems like even with the best laid plans and the careful examination of the expected expenses something comes up that may cause you to require additional funds you had not anticipated. The following are just some possible sources of such funds:

- Borrowing from a bank or other non-disqualified person. Keep in mind that you cannot guarantee the debt so if you are going to incur debt it needs to be non-recourse or guaranteed by a non-disqualified person. A non-recourse loan is one under which the lender has recourse only against the property and not the IRA owner personally.

- Making the maximum allowable annual contributions to the IRA to provide these funds.

- Transfer or rollover funds from other IRA accounts.

- Rollover of funds from your account under an employer 401(k) plan.

Yes, but Can I Buy the Beach House in My IRA?

The answer to this is generally yes but. . . As long as you buy the beach house from a stranger or someone who does not fall under the category of disqualified persons then the purchase is okay. I say beach house because I get asked this question so often but it could be a house in the mountains or at the lake or whatever type of property particularly interests you.

The "but" comes because you cannot use it personally so long as it is held within the IRA. Nor can you rent it to yourself along with others. You can rent it strictly to allowable persons which would be any person who is not a disqualified person, as described in more detail later.

You can also use the beach house **eventually** by taking a distribution of the beach house from your IRA. At that point, you own the property yourself and you can do with it as you please. Keep in mind that the distribution will result in taxable income to you (unless the distribution is from a Roth IRA) equal to the value of the house. Also, the distribution may result in penalties if you are under age 51½.

However, while it is held in your IRA or 401(k) plan account, you need to think of it at any other investment. You cannot use the beach house personally and you cannot personally perform upkeep or improvements to the property. You can rent it but it must be to people who are not prohibited persons. Most importantly, you cannot rent it to yourself or to certain family members who constitute disqualified persons.

Ted has decided to buy a house in the mountains using funds in his IRA. Ted cannot stay in the mountain house or do any work on it so long as it is owned by his IRA. He can rent it out to unrelated parties and when Ted retires he can take a distribution of the mountain house from his IRA, pay the tax (unless, of course, the IRA is a Roth IRA) and from that point forward treat the house as his, including living in the house.

Conclusion

Straightforward investments are the exception rather than the rule. If you find such investment then good for you. However, my experience has been that most of the desirable investments require more cash than you have available in your IRA and/or 401(k). Because of this you are forced into using debt or partnering with others.

Next Chapter

In the next chapter, I will focus on the practical aspects of buying real estate in your IRA or 401(k) plan account. I think you will find this very useful information.

CHAPTER 7

Practicalities of Buying Real Estate in Your IRA

INTRODUCTION

Every administrator is probably going to have slightly different paperwork but I will endeavor in this chapter to give you some generalities which should be of help to you in dealing with any administrator.

LOCATING A DESIRABLE PROPERTY

Your first step in buying a piece of real estate in your IRA or 401(k) plan account is to find a piece of real estate that makes sense. While you may initially be tempted to want to buy anything that comes along, you need to be careful and analyze the cost of buying the asset and the expected returns and make sure you are making a good decision.

Once you have located a desirable piece of real estate, undertake either yourself or through others what is commonly called "due diligence." In this stage you would check out the condition of the real estate, particularly if it involves an existing building. You also want to do some preliminary checking on the title to make sure that the seller of the property will be able to convey clean title to your IRA or 401(k) plan account.

CONTRACT STAGE

You need to be careful that the contract is in the name of your IRA or 401(k) plan account from the beginning. As an example, the purchaser would be "Name of Administrator fbo Your Name IRA."

At least some administrators that I am aware of will not allow you to do an assignment of the contract to your IRA or 401(k) plan account. It is therefore very important to plan ahead and get the contract in the name of the IRA or 401(k) plan account from the beginning and send a copy of the contract with your approval to your administrator.

It is important that you read over the contract, mark it as "read and approved," then send it on to your administrator which will be the party entering into the contract on behalf of your IRA or 401(k) plan account.

Closing Stage

Prior to closing, the administrator must make sure that your IRA or 401(k) plan account name is used on any title insurance or hazard insurance or the like.

Also, as you receive closing documents such as a copy of the closing statement and the deed, all of these should be forwarded on to your administrator. Make sure you read over all of these documents and that you mark them "read and approved" before forwarding them on to your administrator.

All expenses of the closing need to be paid by your IRA or 401(k) plan account which is doing the purchase. These can all be picked up on the closing statement or if you need to pay any expenses in advance, make sure that you correspond with your IRA or 401(k) plan account administrator and have the expenses paid out of your IRA or 401(k) plan account. Do not pay them yourself. The administrator likely will have a form you will need to complete and send in to pay the expenses out of your IRA or 401(k) plan account.

If Your IRA or 401(k) is Obtaining a Loan

If your IRA or 401(k) plan account is going to obtain a loan to purchase the property, then all of the loan documents need to be reviewed by you but they must be set up in the name of your IRA or 401(k) plan account. Once you have reviewed all of the loan documents, you should forward these on to your administrator prior to the closing again marked "read and approved."

Post Closing

Copies of all closing documents should be sent to your administrator. These include the final version of the closing statement, the deed (made out to your IRA or 401(k) plan account), copies of any title policies (again naming your IRA or 401(k) plan account) as well as any hazard insurance policies (again in the name of your IRA or 401(k) plan account).

Next Chapter

The next chapter will give you some guidelines on having your IRA or 401(k) plan account partner with you or others. You may well find that this is the only way you can afford a desirable real estate asset.

CHAPTER 8

More Complex Investments in Real Estate— Teaming Up with Yourself and Others

INTRODUCTION

If you can find a piece of property and have sufficient funds in your IRA or 401(k) plan account to both purchase the property in full for cash and set aside a sufficient reserve to allow for any payments in connection with the property (together with a reserve of extra funds for unexpected expenses), then congratulations to you. This clearly is the optimal situation to be in.

However, often times a desirable property will require more in the way of funds than you have available in your IRA or 401(k), so you are forced to look for other alternatives. Once you do this, you will be entering the world of less straightforward investments. The requirements discussed in Chapter 6 regarding securing an IRA or 401(k) administrator that will allow for investment in real estate as well as purchase from a non-prohibited person still apply. On top of these though you are layering in concerns about sufficiency of money to buy a property that you are really interested in.

Below are some possibilities for you to consider for achieving your goals.

TEAMING UP WITH YOURSELF

One possibility is that your IRA teams up with you to purchase a piece of property. In order to do this, you cannot use your IRA or the property in it as security to obtain funds that you would use to make the investment. You must come up with the funds separately.

It is permissible for you to use indebtedness secured by property that you own outside your IRA to provide funds for this purpose. For example, you could borrow funds secured by your primary residence and use these funds to invest along with funds held in your IRA in a commercial property. In this scenario you and your IRA would each own undivided interests or you would purchase the property together with your IRA through ownership of an LLC or other entity.

In the latter case, you and your IRA would each own an interest in the LLC or other entity and you and your IRA would each contribute funds in proportion to your ownership interest. The LLC or other entity would then actually own the property that you desired to purchase, with you and your IRA owning the LLC or other entity.

For example, Tom wants to buy a fast food restaurant having a purchase price of $500,000. He has only $300,000 in his IRA and must come up with the other $200,000. Tom borrows the $200,000 against his principal residence and then partners with his IRA to purchase the restaurant. The IRA owns 60% of the investment and would receive 60% of any net income. Tom owns the other 40% directly and would receive 40% of the net income. Tom will be personally responsible for any payments on the mortgage loan secured by his principal residence.

One advantage of obtaining the loan yourself outside of your IRA is that you can deduct the interest and depreciation which would not be a great advantage to the IRA which is generally a tax exempt entity. Keep in mind however that you will only be receiving part of the rent so you may not be receiving enough to cover your loan payments.

TEAMING UP WITH OTHERS

Any time you begin bringing in other people you have the prospects for problems to develop. However, you may be forced to look at this possibility to come up with the necessary funds to purchase a really desirable property. If you do not have sufficient funds yourself or cannot borrow these then you would be put in the position of having to find third parties to invest along with your IRA.

The investment by these third parties can be co-ownership in the form of co-tenancies or through entities such as limited liability companies. Having your IRA and others (or their IRAs) own the property as co-tenants raises problems in that all of the owners would have to agree on a number of items, including a sale of the property. Any time you have to get the agreement of a number of several parties, this can be difficult and time consuming.

If you are looking at the possibility of buying a property with others through a co-tenancy arrangement be sure to have an agreement which spells out to the owners what vote would be required for a sale or on other important decisions, such as maintenance.

If you go the route of working with others through an entity such as an LLC, then the various investors would contribute money in exchange for membership interests in the LLC or other entity. The funds contributed to the LLC or other entity (together with any debt secured by the property) would be used by the LLC or other entity to purchase the desired property. The property would be held in the name of the LLC or other entity.

Finally, anytime you are looking at an investment with others, you will need to be aware of the prohibited transaction rules and the Plan Asset Rules. The prohibited transaction rules are discussed more in later chapters. The Plan Asset Rules also are discussed at greater length later but basically these rules involve looking through an entity to the underlying assets and treating those underlying assets as if owned directly by the IRA or 401(k) plan.

INVESTING WITH OTHERS THROUGH A CO-TENANCY OR AN LLC OR OTHER ENTITY

One of the most common ways for investments to be made by IRAs and qualified plan accounts is through an entity such as an LLC which then invests in a property. Because investments through an entity such as an LLC have become so common, there will be a separate discussion of this form of investment below. There also is the possibility of investment with others through a tenancy in common arrangement, which is far less common.

CO-TENANCY OR TENANTS IN COMMON

You can enter into an investment with other parties as tenants in common but there are some disadvantages to the tenancy in common. Because each of the owners owns an undivided interest in the property, it takes the agreement (absent a written agreement to the contrary) of all of the co-owners to sell the property.

Before considering entering into a co-tenancy or ownership as tenants in common, there should be a written agreement among the various co-tenants regarding what sort of vote would be required for major actions such as sale, refinance of any indebtedness of the co-tenants and maintenance of the property. Because of the title and other complications created by ownership with tenancy in common, you will rarely see this type of ownership. More likely ownership will be through an LLC or other entity as described below.

LLCs

Various types of entities, including a partnership or a corporation, can be used but in my experience the most common entity of choice has become the limited liability company or LLC. This is because the LLC combines many of the asset protection features of the corporation—unlike the limited partnership which must have a general partner who will be liable for the debts of the entity, the LLC does not have to have any member who has personal liability for debts of the organization—while also affording the often beneficial tax treatment afforded to partnerships. Partnerships and LLCs are what are commonly referred to as pass-through entities. This means that instead of the income or loss of the LLC being taxable to the entity, the items of income and loss of the LLC (or partnership) are passed through to its owners who then pick up these items on their personal returns.

The following diagram may be of help to you in visualizing the IRA ownership of an interest in the LLC while the LLC owns the property.

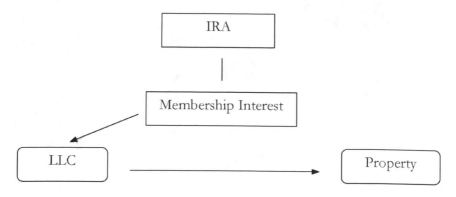

The use of an LLC owned by an IRA is an area of particular concern to the regulatory authorities such as the Federal Deposit Insurance Corporation and Internal Revenue Service. Because of the scrutiny, the administrators are adding extra requirements in the event you want to use an LLC. Your administrator likely will require a number of things from you, including an attorney's opinion letter that there are no prohibited transactions being committed upon the setting up of the LLC, and an annual evaluation of any real estate owned by the LLC and other paperwork. For this reason, you may determine that the LLC is more trouble than it is worth.

USE OF DEBT

Although this topic is discussed in greater detail later, basically your IRA or 401(k) can incur debt to purchase a more valuable asset. However, that debt must be non-recourse or the debt must be guaranteed by a person who is not prohibited.

NEXT CHAPTER

If you have read through this chapter carefully, you may well have reached the conclusion that any sort of ownership with third parties is probably more trouble than you want to get involved in. An alternative to this is the use of debt by your IRA or 401(k) plan account in purchasing the real estate asset. The subject of debt is very important and is discussed in the next chapter.

CHAPTER 9

Use of Debt in Investments by Your IRA or 401(k) Plan Account

INTRODUCTION

Rarely do things work out so simply that your IRA or 401(k) can just pay cash for the property you want unless you have a considerable amount of cash in your IRA. More often, to obtain a valuable property, you will be looking at debt to augment the cash to purchase the property.

Keep in mind that not only do you need to have enough cash for the purchase of the property but you also need to make sure there is enough cash in the account to pay operating expenses, including mortgage payments, in excess of whatever rent you may be receiving for the property. You will also need to have sufficient funds set aside for unexpected expenses.

GENERAL RULES

I'm frequently asked about the rules relating to when you can use debt in connection with investments by an IRA or qualified plan [such as a 401(k)]. This is still another area in which the rules are very complex. The consequences for violating these rules are likely to be a prohibited transaction resulting in the loss of the exempt status of the IRA or qualified plan, so making sure that you navigate these rules correctly is very important.

There are at least three different areas which each have their own unique sets of rules:

1. An investment made by only your IRA, 401(k) plan account or other qualified plan account;

2. An investment made by your IRA, 401(k) account or other qualified plan account along with you or some other disqualified person (such as your spouse, parent or a child, or various entities in which you own a 50% or more in interest); and

3. An investment by your IRA or qualified plan account in an entity such as a limited liability company ("LLC") where it is the LLC or other entity that is seeking to use debt in connection with an investment by the company.

Each of these three general areas will be dealt with below. I also will touch on what constitutes non-recourse debt. Regardless of the type of investments that you find yourself in, this would be relevant to your considerations. As an alternative, if non-recourse debt is not readily available then you can look at a debt guaranteed by a non-disqualified person.

INVESTMENT 100% OWNED BY IRA OR QUALIFIED PLAN

An IRA, 401(k) plan account or other qualified plan account may borrow funds that it uses in connection with an investment as long as the debt is used for the benefit of the IRA and not for the benefit of the owner of the IRA. In other words, the IRA could not borrow money that was used to allow the IRA owner to purchase a home.

In addition, the loan generally must be non-recourse (or guaranteed by an allowable person as discussed below) so that, if the IRA or qualified plan defaults, the lender has recourse only to those assets of the IRA or qualified plan which are security for the loan. This means the lender cannot come back against you as the owner of the plan. You cannot guarantee the loan without engaging in a prohibited transaction which would disqualify the IRA or qualified plan.

Given the relative reluctance of lenders to deal with loans in general in the current economic environment, it may be very difficult to find a lender that will allow your IRA to obtain a non-recourse loan.

If non-recourse debt is not readily available, then it is possible to have the debt guaranteed. The debt could be guaranteed by persons who do not fall within the disqualified person category. For example, you could have a business associate guaranty the loan. You clearly could not guaranty the loan yourself. Nor could your spouse or parent or lineal descendent. A discussion of prohibited persons who could not guarantee the loan is contained in a later chapter.

Finding someone to guarantee a loan who is not a prohibited person is not easy. In order to induce a true third party to guarantee the loan you are probably looking at having to pay the person something to provide the guarantee. Given this, obtaining guaranteed loans may be difficult and costly.

An alternative is to have a loan guaranteed by family members who do not fall within the list of prohibited persons. As an example, the loan could be guaranteed by a brother or sister but could not be guaranteed by a parent or a child. Hopefully, these people would not be looking to receive a fee for providing the guarantee, but that is obviously a point for discussion between the IRA owner and the related party.

SELLER FINANCED PROPERTIES

Perhaps the easiest debt to deal with is if the seller of a property is willing to take back a promissory note as part of the purchase price. This form of debt is clearly permissible for IRAs and 401(k) plans (assuming, of course, the seller is not a prohibited person) and is often times the easiest and cheapest to obtain. Typically, the seller would have recourse only against the property in the event of a default in payments under the promissory note.

INVESTMENT BY YOU TOGETHER WITH YOUR IRA OR QUALIFIED PLAN USING DEBT

This is an area where it gets more difficult to make anything work but with careful planning you can pursue a strategy that is perfectly permissible in this area.

If there is a loan to the IRA for a deal in which you have also invested personally, then this is regarded as a prohibited transaction because the IRA is regarded as incurring a debt for your benefit (i.e., with respect to the part of the investment made by you, personally). You could borrow the funds personally needed to make the investment with your IRA or qualified plan, but the IRA or qualified plan cannot in any way be involved in the loan and you cannot use the property being purchased by the IRA as security for a loan obtained by you.

What is perfectly permissible, though, is for you to obtain a loan secured by your own assets (excluding the IRA and any property held by it) and then using those funds together with funds supplied by your IRA to purchase a property. For example, you could borrow money secured by your principal residence and use that money to enter into an investment along with your IRA or qualified plan. You and the IRA would then own property either as tenants in common or you could take title through a limited liability company or other entity.

INCURRING DEBT THROUGH AN LLC

In the case of ownership of the property by an LLC, typically, the LLC can obtain a loan secured by the property owned by the LLC. This property is not an asset of the IRA or qualified plan. Rather the ownership of an interest in the LLC is the asset of the IRA or qualified plan. Be aware, this general statement is subject to a number of exceptions which are touched on below. Although the same concept applies to other entities in addition to the LLC, my experience has been that the LLC has become the vehicle of choice.

ALLOWABLE DEBT

There are real disagreements among even the so-called experts in terms of exactly how these rules would be applied in particular situations. Moreover, the whole discussion has gotten more complicated by the positions being taken by the IRS and later the DOL (Department of Labor) which seem to indicate a trend toward the government saying that even if you fit within the rules and, therefore, have not committed a prohibited transaction, the government may decide that they do not like a transaction so it was in effect a prohibited transaction even if not literally covered by the rules.

Having said this, investors and syndicators should not stay away from this area simply out of fear of the Plan Asset Rules. So long as you are aware of these rules and plan accordingly, a transaction can be done which is perfectly legal.

EXCEPTIONS

Some of the exceptions to the allowability of incurring debt through an LLC or other entity are as follows:

1. If you and your IRA own 100% of an LLC or other entity, then the assets will be treated as if owned directly by you and your IRA. You would be thrown back into the rules regulating investments by you together with your IRA or qualified plan. As discussed above, the LLC likely will not be able to incur a debt in this case.

2. If you own 50% or more of an LLC or other entity, then the entity becomes a disqualified person and any transactions between your IRA and the entity would constitute a prohibited transaction. It would be allowable for you and your IRA to purchase more than a 50% interest in an LLC in a single transaction (as long as the purchase is not from a prohibited person). A common strategy is to have you and your IRA purchase a 50% or greater interest in a new LLC, which is perfectly permissible. Again, a potential problem here is, if the LLC incurs a debt, you run into the same

54

situation of the debt being regarded as having been incurred for your benefit.

3. If you and your IRA or qualified plan owns less than 100% of an LLC or other entity the next question is whether the entity comes within the Plan Asset Rules. If the entity is subject to the Plan Asset Rules, then the assets of the LLC can be treated as being owned pro rata by the IRA based on its percentage membership interest in the company. A couple of thoughts here may be of help:

   A. If all IRAs or qualified plans together own 25% of the interests in an LLC or other entity (with this computation being complicated by the exclusion of your interest in the LLC under certain circumstances), then the assets of the LLC or other entity are treated as owned pro-rata by the IRAs and qualified plans.

   B. What this means as a practical matter is that unless you fall within an exception to the Plan Asset Rules, any transactions between you and the LLC will be viewed in the same way as if you were doing the transaction directly with your IRA.

   C. Also, if the LLC has incurred debt, the debt is no longer considered the debt of the LLC, but the debt of the IRA investing in the LLC. If you are also individually an investor in the LLC then you likely have a problem with this debt because it will be regarded as having been incurred by the IRA for your benefit.

   D. However, even if you do fall within the Plan Asset Rules on a technical percentage basis, you may have an argument that you are nonetheless exempt from these rules because you qualify under one of the exceptions. The most common exception that we encounter is the one for a real estate operating company. The Plan Asset Rules and the exceptions from such rules are discussed in greater detail in a later chapter.

If you do somehow run afoul of these rules, you must be careful in entering into transactions with the LLC so that you do not violate the prohibited transaction rules. If you do run afoul of the prohibited transaction rules, then your IRA or qualified plan will be disqualified and you may face penalties.

Do not despair though because even if you become subject to the Plan Assets Rules, through careful planning you can still avoid committing a prohibited transaction.

The consequences to the syndicator of an LLC running afoul of the Plan Asset Rules are that the syndicator will then be regarded as a fiduciary with respect to the IRAs investing in the LLC. However, there are ways the syndicator can reach agreements with the IRAs prior to the time they become members of the LLC which should be acceptable.

How Would Anyone Know These Complex Rules Have Been Violated?

You may ask how anyone would ever figure out that you had violated one of these rules. The answer is that it likely would come up in the context of an Internal Revenue Service audit of the return related to the IRA or qualified plan or a tax return of an entity in which the IRA or qualified plan was investing. If it does, it might be years after the prohibited transaction had occurred that you would find out that your plan had been disqualified and you would owe the penalties plus interest for having committed a prohibited transaction.

Conclusion: A Lack of Certainty

As indicated above, possibly the most troubling aspect of all with respect to these rules is that, while they are not only exceedingly complex in their own right, there seems to be an increasing willingness by the government to say that, even if you have not technically violated the rules, they may say you violated them simply because they do not like something that you may have done. This often comes about because the government feels that you somehow benefited by a transaction that your IRA or 401(k) was involved in. This means that there will be a lack of certainty and security in this area for some time to come.

Your use of debt in an LLC will simply depend upon your risk tolerance but clearly, to be safe, you would want to be careful about any ownership of an LLC that would bring you under the Plan Asset Rules.

However, having said that, becoming subject to the Plan Asset Rules is not the end of the world but simply has consequences that must be taken into account. I am aware that many syndicators and other tax professionals try to keep investment by IRAs and qualified plans under 25% so as to stay clear of the Plan Asset Rules. I would submit that while this is a worthwhile objective, it is often times not realistic. Becoming subject to the Plan Asset Rules is not necessarily fatal to the transaction.

Not having a substantial IRA or 401(k) investment in an LLC because of the Plan Asset Rules may overlook a very significant market and the LLCs owned primarily by IRAs and 401(k)s are not necessarily an undesirable thing.

My Advice

My best advice for navigating these complex rules is to either have your IRA own real estate assets and use a non-recourse loan to finance this, or partner with your IRA or 401(k) yourself. In this latter case, you can borrow the funds personally as long as you secure the loan with assets other than the IRA or its property.

Next Chapter

After alluding to the prohibited transaction rules a number of times in this book, the next chapter will take you into the world of the prohibited transactions and will equip you to avoid them. If you want to pursue investments in real estate, you need to be aware of the prohibited transaction rules. It is easy to avoid prohibited transactions if you know what you are doing. The next chapter will equip you with that knowledge.

CHAPTER 10

Prohibited Transactions—What Not to do With Your IRA

LEARNING TO NOT OVERLY FEAR PROHIBITED TRANSACTIONS

Experience has taught me that people seem to be petrified at the thought of committing a prohibited transaction with their IRA or 401(k) plan account. Given the penalties, I can understand this.

However, it's important to understand the concepts involved because fear of a prohibited transaction can lead you to ignore a perfectly permissible investment. There are plenty of transactions out there that can produce significant returns that do not involve prohibited transactions. In order to search out these transactions, you need to know what constitutes a prohibited transaction.

WHAT ARE PROHIBITED TRANSACTIONS?

A prohibited transaction normally is a transaction between the IRA [or 401(k) account] and a disqualified person. The following may be of help to you in visualizing a prohibited transaction.

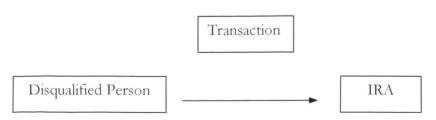

Some examples of prohibited transactions are listed below. For ease of reference, transactions with IRAs only will be discussed but the same rules apply to a 401(k) account.

1. A transfer of IRA income or assets to, or use of them by or for the benefit of, a disqualified person. The key here is who is a disqualified person. This is because "the transfer of assets or the use of them by or for the benefit" is so broad that it encompasses virtually everything.

    The most commonly disqualified person is you. From my experience, the most common prohibited transaction is a sale of assets you already own to your IRA. As an example, Joe owns a trailer park. He has decided that the burdens of owning the trailer park personally are too much and wishes he had bought the trailer park through his IRA instead. Joe wants to sell the trailer park to his IRA, but to do so would be a prohibited transaction.

2. Among the activities between an IRA and a disqualified person that can result in a prohibited transaction include:
    a. Selling, exchanging or leasing property;
    b. Lending money, extending credit; or
    c. Furnishing goods, services or facilities.

Again, the key becomes who is a disqualified person.

3. Dealing with IRA income or assets by a fiduciary for his or her own interest. As long as you choose a true third party fiduciary, you are less likely to run afoul of these rules since the fiduciary will be aware of the prohibited transaction rules and will make sure it does not violate them.

4. The receiving of consideration by a fiduciary for his or her own account from a party that is dealing with the IRA in a transaction that involves IRA income or assets. One example of this would be someone working for your IRA administrator who took a payment personally for helping the IRA find an investment. This should not be an issue in most cases.

The list of disqualified persons set forth below is straight out of the IRS rules. In my opinion, the most commonly disqualified persons who enter into transactions with your IRA are you and certain of your relatives. Because of this, transactions with family members are dealt with separately.

It becomes crucial to learn who are disqualified persons and who are not disqualified persons. I say this because any time you have a transaction between a disqualified person and an IRA, you likely will have a prohibited transaction.

Other commentators have different categories of prohibited transactions, but I think if you focus on the transactions between disqualified persons and an IRA or qualified plan, you will have discovered the vast bulk of prohibited transactions.

WHO ARE DISQUALIFIED PERSONS?

Disqualified persons generally are the following:

1. You;
2. An employer of any participants in the IRA;
3. A 10% (or more) partner in a partnership having an IRA;
4. A fiduciary of the IRA;
5. A highly compensated employee (earning 10% or more of the employer's yearly wages);
6. An employee organization, any of whose members are covered by the IRA;
7. A person providing services to the IRA;
8. Certain members of your family (the treatment of family members is dealt with in more detail below); or
9. Corporations, partnerships, trusts, or estate in which you own, directly or indirectly, at least half the:
   a. Total voting stock or the value of all stock of the corporation,
   b. Capital interest or profit interest of the partnership, or
   c. Beneficial interest of the trust or estate.

TRANSACTIONS WITH FAMILY MEMBERS

Not all transactions with family are prohibited because not all family members are disqualified. Family members who are disqualified persons who normally come up are your spouse and your children and your parents. Certain family members such as brothers and sisters are not disqualified persons.

The following chart provides a summary of who is disqualified and who is not disqualified among your family members:

Family Members Who Are Disqualified Persons	Family Members Who are not Disqualified Persons, i.e., persons that your IRA can enter into a transaction with
You	Your brothers and sisters
Your spouse	Your spouse's brothers and sisters
Your natural parents and/or your adoptive parents	Your spouse's parents
Your natural grandparents	Your spouse's grandparents
Your natural children and/or your adopted children	Your stepchildren
The spouses of your natural children	Your spouse's stepchildren
	Your aunts, uncles, and cousins

You might keep this chart handy anytime you are considering a transaction between your IRA and a family member.

Picking up the example of Joe again, Joe could also not sell the trailer park to the IRA of his parents or the IRA of his children. However, he could sell the trailer park to an IRA owned by his brothers or sisters.

PENALTIES FOR PROHIBITED TRANSACTIONS

If someone other than the owner or beneficiary of an IRA engages in a prohibited transaction with respect to an IRA, that person may be liable for certain excise taxes, generally a 15% tax on the amount of the prohibited transaction. This is followed by a 100% additional tax if the transaction is not corrected.

If the owner or beneficiary of an IRA engages in a prohibited transaction with respect to the IRA, then the IRA loses its exempt status and the owner or beneficiary (as applicable) must include the fair market value of the IRA assets in gross income for the year of the prohibited transaction.

EXEMPTIONS

There are a number of exemptions from the prohibited transaction rules, but I will not address them in this book.

CONCLUSION

As you can see, the penalties for a prohibited transaction are severe but the actual scope of prohibited transactions is relatively narrow. Given this, you should not be so scared of committing a prohibited transaction as to limit your investments to traditional ones. Instead, you need to develop a working knowledge of what actually constitutes a prohibited transaction so you can avoid committing one.

There are plenty of investment opportunities out there in real estate which do not involve prohibited transactions. For example, as long as the transaction is entered into with a stranger such as a purchase of land from a true third party, you will not run afoul of the prohibited transaction rules.

Next Chapter

Now that you know what a prohibited transaction is, the next step in your IRA education is to understand the concept of unrelated business taxable income. As you will learn in the next chapter, unrelated business taxable income can result in some income to your IRA but it is not necessarily a bad thing. Turn to the next chapter to learn about this important concept.

CHAPTER 11

Unrelated Business Taxable Income:
Is it a Bad Thing?

WHY SHOULD I BE CONCERNED ABOUT THIS?

While unrelated business taxable income ("UBTI") does not cause your IRA (or in some limited cases your other qualified plan) to lose its exempt status, the rules can cause income to be taxable to your IRA or possibly your qualified plan. As you are probably already aware, the income from an IRA or other qualified plan typically is not taxable. However, UBTI realized by an IRA can be taxable.

While generating some taxable income certainly is not fatal to any investment you are considering, it is part of the considerations you need to make in assessing any investment. If an investment is making money, then the fact that you have to pay some tax on it is not necessarily a bad thing. You simply have to factor the cost of the UBTI into your analysis when considering whether to undertake an investment through your IRA or some other way.

WHAT CONSTITUTES UBTI?

Discussing this whole area reminds me of starting down a highway and after having gone several miles coming to a sign that tells you to make an immediate u-turn because you are headed in the wrong direction. What I mean by this is that the UBTI rules exclude rents but then say the exclusion may not apply if you have debt-financed property. Therefore, you generally are subject to the UBTI rules if you have any debt-financed property even if you have otherwise passive income like rents. Perhaps the best way to approach the UBTI rules is to understand the policy considerations that give rise to these rules.

The UBTI rules were put in place to keep tax-exempt organizations from competing with for-profit taxpaying businesses. Therefore, its most obvious intent was to tax an otherwise exempt organization on the income it received from running a business in competition with taxable business entities.

Consistent with this intent, the general rule under the Code is that the income from a trade or business which is not substantially related to the organization's charitable, educational or other purpose or function will be taxable. Since IRAs do not really have an exempt purpose other than their existence as a retirement vehicle, any business conducted by an IRA is likely to be regarded as an unrelated trade or business.

However, since the goal of the UBTI rules was to prevent tax-exempt organizations from having a competitive advantage over taxable businesses in operating an active business, passive income is generally not subject to UBTI. Included within passive income are interest and dividends as well as royalties.

Also, included as passive income and hence excluded from UBTI are rents from real property as long as (i) the rent is not determined based upon the income or profits of the property and (ii) there is no excessive rendering of services in connection with the real estate investment.

This exception which excludes rents from real property from being treated as unrelated business taxable income does not apply if more than 50% of the total rent received under a lease is attributable to personal property. Moreover, the rents for personal property leased with real property where the rents attributable to the personal property are an incidental amount of the total amount received is not unrelated business taxable income. What this means is that if you have some personal property that is being used with real property but the lease payments for the personal property are relatively small in comparison to the rent for the real estate, then the rents for the personal property are not unrelated business taxable income.

Finally, the sale of a property is not subject to UBTI unless it constitutes stock in trade or property held primarily for sale to customers in the ordinary course of a trade or business.

However, having said this, all of these rules go by the wayside and you are back to having UBTI if you have debt financed income.

Debt-Financed Property

Who Needs To Be Concerned About These Rules?

While most rents are exempt from UBTI, there is a very large exception from these rules. The operating income as well as possibly the gain or loss on the sale of a property becomes taxable to the extent that there is acquisition indebtedness with respect to the property.

As to who should be concerned by these rules, it is very clear that IRAs are subject to the tax on debt-financed income. Most qualified plans, including 401(k)s, are not subject to the tax on debt-financed income so long as the indebtedness qualifies under certain rules. For more on that, see "Debt Financed Property Rules as They Apply to 401(k)s and Other Qualified Plans" at the end of this chapter.

What Income Is Subject To Tax?

A certain amount of the operating income from a property with respect to which there is acquisition indebtedness becomes taxable. In addition, a certain amount of the gain or loss on the sale of property with respect to which there has been acquisition indebtedness with respect to the property during the 12 months prior to its sale is taxable. The method for determining the amount which is taxable is described below. The operating income is taxable for the life of the investment while the gain on the sale is taxable only upon the sale.

How Bad Is It To Be Subject To the Debt-Financed Income Rules?

Unlike the drastic consequences for violating the prohibited transaction rules, essentially nothing terribly bad happens to your IRA if it has acquisition indebtedness, other than that a portion of the operating income and possibly the gain on the sale of the property becomes taxable. Your IRA is not disqualified and you are not subject to any penalty taxes.

You simply need as part of your analysis of a potential property acquisition to take into account the income tax cost of the investment. In many cases you will find that even after paying the tax the investment still makes very good sense. Accordingly, do not dismiss an investment out of hand simply because it may generate debt-financed income.

For example, Joe has decided to purchase an apartment building through his IRA which will generate $50,000 per year. He will finance 50% of the purchase price with a mortgage in the name of his IRA. His IRA will fund the other 50% with cash. In this example, 50% of the net income to Joe's IRA would be taxable as unrelated business taxable income. Joe would simply need to determine whether after his IRA pays the taxes on this income he is still getting enough income to make the investment worthwhile for his IRA.

WHAT IS ACQUISITION INDEBTEDNESS?

Glad you have asked. Acquisition indebtedness is debt incurred to either purchase or improve a piece of real property held to produce income. Specifically, acquisition indebtedness includes all of the following:

- Indebtedness incurred by the IRA in acquiring or improving a property;

- Indebtedness incurred before the acquisition or improvement of the property if the indebtedness would not have been incurred but for the acquisition or improvement; and

- Indebtedness incurred after the acquisition or improvement of the property, if the indebtedness would not have been incurred but for the acquisition or improvement and the incurrence of the indebtedness was reasonably foreseeable at the time of the acquisition or improvement.

It is usually pretty obvious that debt incurred at the time of the acquisition or improvement of a piece of property by an IRA constitutes acquisition indebtedness.

The complicating factor would come if the IRA borrowed further money later, not directly related to the acquisition or improvement of the property, but which arguably could have been foreseen at the time of the acquisition.

My feeling is that as a practical matter it is going to be difficult for an IRA to borrow money unless it is directly related to real estate or some other asset acquisition. Lenders are going to be reluctant to lend money to an IRA unless it is directly related to a piece of real property owned by the IRA.

Moreover, any extension, renewal or refinancing of acquisition indebtedness continues to be treated as acquisition indebtedness. In addition, if an IRA sells property without paying off the acquisition indebtedness and then buys property that is otherwise not debt-financed property, the unpaid debt is treated as acquisition indebtedness with respect to the new property even if the original property is not debt-financed property.

If there is a debt incurred in part to purchase or improve a piece of real property and there is other debt that is incurred by the IRA for some other purpose, then only the percentage of the total debt that is acquisition indebtedness causes the income and gain to be taxable to the IRA. For example, let's say an IRA purchases a property and borrows $100,000 to purchase and/or undertake improvements to the property, and then later borrows an additional $100,000 secured by the property but unrelated to the purchase or improvements. Then, only a maximum of 50% of the income and gain with respect to the property is going to be subject to the tax on debt-financed property.

How Much of the Gross Operating Income Is Subject To Tax?

If you determine that you do have acquisition indebtedness with respect to a piece of real property, then a percentage of the income from this property becomes taxable annually. The percentage is based on a formula of the average acquisition indebtedness divided by the average adjusted basis. Here's the simple computation formula:

$$\frac{\text{Average acquisition indebtedness}}{\text{Average adjusted basis}} \quad X \quad \text{Gross income from debt-financed property}$$

The following definitions may help you in looking at this:

Average Acquisition Indebtedness:

You take the amount of acquisition indebtedness as of the first day of each month during the taxable year in which the IRA owns the property, add those up and then divide by the total number of months during the year the IRA owned the property (i.e., if the IRA owns the property for the whole year, then you add up the acquisition indebtedness on the first day of each of the twelve months of the year and then divide the sum by 12).

Average Adjusted Basis:

To compute this, you add the basis on the first day of the tax year the IRA owned the property and the basis on the last day of the year (or the last day the IRA owns the property during the year) and divide that by 2.

You then apply this percentage to the gross operating income from the property to come up with the amount of the gross income which is potentially subject to tax that taxable year. You then need to take into account the allowable deductions summarized below.

The following is an example taken largely from the Regulations that may be of help to you in applying these rules.

> On July 7, an IRA buys an office building for $510,000 using $300,000 of borrowed funds. During the year the only adjustment to basis is $20,000 for depreciation. Starting July 28, the IRA pays $20,000 each month on the mortgage principal and interest. The debt/basis percentage for the year is calculated as follows:

Debt on first day of each month property is held

July	$300,000
August	$280,000
September	$260,000
October	$240,000
November	$220,000
December	$200,000
TOTAL:	<u>$1,500,000</u>

Avg. acquisition indebtedness:
$1,500,000 ÷ 6 months   <u>$250,000</u>

	Basis
As of July 7	$510,000
As of December 31	$490,000
Total:	$1,000,000

Avg. Adjusted Basis:
$1,000,000 ÷ 2 months $500,000

Debt/basis percentage:
$250,000 ÷ $500,000   = 50%

WHAT DEDUCTIONS ARE ALLOWABLE?

In computing the net amount taxable, certain deductions from gross income are available:

1. Only the expenses directly connected with the debt-financed property are deductible from the allocated gross income. The normal sorts of deductions that you would incur with respect to any real estate investment such as insurance, taxes, interest and maintenance expenses would be deductible.
2. In computing the deductions, if the property is depreciable, then depreciation must be computed on a straight line basis only.

Under the straight line basis, the cost of the property would be divided by the number of years in its useful life as dictated by the IRS. You can only deduct the same fixed amount every year.

3. In addition, once you come up with the allowable deductions and straight line depreciation amount, then only the percentage which corresponds to the gross income percentage calculated above is allowed as a deduction.

4. Finally, once you calculate the operating income after the deductions, then the IRA is allowed a $1,000.00 per year specific deduction to come up with its taxable income for the year. Since the IRA's income is going to be exempt, other than that related to debt-financed property, then the income attributable to the debt-financed property should constitute the full amount of the IRA's taxable income.

What Are the Tax Rates That Apply To the Net Debt-Financed Income?

The income of the IRA is subject to tax at the normal trust income tax rules which climb fairly steeply. In 2009 the tax rates were as follows:

If your taxable income is:		The tax is:	
Over:	But not over:		Of the amount over:
$0	$2,300	.... 15%	$0
2,300	5,350	$345.00 + 25%	2,300
5,350	8,200	1,107.50 + 28%	5,350
8,200	11,150	1,905.50 + 33%	8,200
11,150	....	2,879.00 + 35%	11,150

All This Is Complicated—Can You Give Me a Simple Step-By-Step Example?

Here's a practical approach to calculating the portion of the operating income from a debt-financed property that is subject to tax:

First, calculate the net operating income from the property. Although all of the Regulations and IRS publications speak in terms of computing the gross income and the allowable deductions separately, I think when it comes to an IRA investing in real estate, it is safe enough to just compute the net operating income. You would do this as follows:

A. Calculate the gross income from the property.

B. Calculate the deductions directly connected with the property. Obviously mortgage interest, utilities, insurance on the property and property management fees should qualify as directly connected.

C. Calculate the depreciation on a straight line basis.

Now deduct the directly connected deductions and the straight line depreciation from the gross income to come up with a net income figure.

Second, calculate the percentage of the net operating income that is taxable based on the amount of the acquisition indebtedness in relation to the basis of the property. The following is a shorthand summary of how you compute it:

$$\frac{\text{Average acquisition indebtedness}}{\text{Average adjusted basis}} \quad \mathbf{X} \quad \text{Net income from debt-financed property}$$

- Acquisition indebtedness: - debt incurred to purchase or improve real estate property as discussed further above
- Average indebtedness: - first of each month ÷ 12.
- Average basis: - first and last of days of year ÷ 2.

The basic details of this are as follows:

A. Calculate the amount owed on the acquisition indebtedness as of the first day of each month of the year the IRA owns the real estate (unless it is the year of purchase or sale this will be 12 months). The monthly principal balance of the debt should be able to be picked up from an amortization statement.

B. Divide this amount by 12.

C. Compute the average basis. Basically you just take the basis on the first and last days of the year (or the day the property is purchased or the date it is sold in the year of purchase or sale) and then divide by 2.

D. This will give you the numerator and denominator by which you multiply the net operating income to come up with the portion that is taxable.

Third, once you come up with the portion of the income that is taxable, you deduct $1,000. This is a set rule under Code § 512 that the $1,000 is in lieu of other exemptions.

Fourth, once you determine the actual taxable income from the property less the $1,000, you then need to apply the trust tax rates. This assumes that the operating income from the debt-financed property is the only taxable income that the IRA has. In the usual case this is true and the only question will be how many debt financed properties the IRA owns. The 2009 trust rates are summarized above.

How Is the IRA's Gain on the Sale of the Property Taxed?

If your IRA sells a property that is subject to acquisition indebtedness or was subject to acquisition indebtedness at any time during the 12 months prior to its sale, then the gain or loss from the sale becomes taxable in accordance with the normal tax rules (meaning that it may be a capital gain or loss depending upon whether the IRA has held the property for a year). The amount of the gain or loss which will be subject to tax is based upon a percentage equal to the highest acquisition indebtedness ratio during the prior 12 months in relation to the property's average adjusted basis. In other words, the percentage of the gain on the sale of the property is based upon the amount of the acquisition indebtedness in relation to the tax basis of the property. The only wrinkle here is that you take the highest percentage of the last 12 months in coming up with how much of the gain is taxable. An example that might help explain this complicated concept follows.

Here's an example taken largely out of the Regulations that may be of help in applying these rules. This example is based on the same facts described in the above example for operating income.

Basis

As of July 10, 1970	$510,000 (acquisition date)
December 31, 1970	$490,000
Total:	$1,000,000

Avg. Adjusted Basis:
$1,000,000 ÷ 2 months   = $500,000

Debt/basis percentage:
Highest acquisition indebtedness
$300,000 ÷ $500,000 = 60%

Turning back to our example of Joe, let us assume that the loan was interest only and so 50% of the purchase price constitutes acquisition indebtedness. Joe would simply need to plug in the amount of the mortgage into the formula above to determine how much of the gain realized by his IRA on the sale of the apartments would be taxable.

If an IRA generates gross unrelated business taxable income of more than $1,000 it must file Form 990-T. It also must make quarterly estimated tax payments computed using Form 990-W.

Debt Financed Property Rules as They Apply To 401(k)s and Other Qualified Plans

As discussed briefly above, most qualified plans, including 401(k)s, are not subject to the tax on debt financed income so long as the indebtedness qualifies under the following points:

- The acquisition price for the property is fixed as of the date of purchase.

- The debt is third party debt and not financed by the seller, a person related to the seller, or a person related to the plan. If any of these people do provide financing then it must be on "commercially reasonable terms." Because of that vagueness, it is probably best to stay away from seller or related party financing.

- Payments on the debt are not based upon the income or profits from the property.

- The property is not leased back to the seller or a person related to the seller.

- The property is not leased back to a person related to the plan.

- The purchaser is not a partnership in which the plan is a partner together with taxable persons where the allocations are designed to avoid tax.

While this is quite a list of exceptions, the reality is that most real estate acquisitions by 401(k)s or qualified plans can avoid them and, therefore, avoid the tax on unrelated business taxable income related to acquisition indebtedness.

In most cases, this means that only IRAs will be really concerned about the debt-financed property rules. Qualified plans such as 401(k) plans will not be as concerned about these rules unless, of course, they fall within one of the exceptions that would put them back into the debt-financed income rules. If you have a 401(k) plan or other qualified plan, you simply need to analyze each real estate investment that involves debt to make sure it is not subject to these rules, or, if it is, to calculate the cost to the plan.

Turning back to Joe once again, if he had made the purchase through a

401(k) plan account rather than an IRA, then he likely would not have been concerned with the unrelated business taxable income rules.

WHAT IS THE BOTTOM LINE ON DEBT-FINANCED INCOME?

Don't dismiss properties out of hand because they may result in debt-financed income. You need to do a careful analysis in assessing a property to see whether it may still make sense to go ahead with the purchase. This is particularly true if you have a plan to pay down the acquisition indebtedness prior to the time your IRA sells the property.

A further useful analysis is to compare the cost of the investment within an IRA to the cost of undertaking the investment outside of the IRA. The following is the 2009 Rate Schedule for persons married filing jointly which may give you some basis for comparison (understanding that these are the most favorable tax rates that can apply to individuals):

If your taxable income is:		The tax is:	
Over:	But not over:		Of the amount over:
$0	$16,700	.... 10%	$0
16,700	67,900	$1,670.00 + 15%	16,700
67,900	137,050	9,350.00 + 25%	67,900
137,050	208,850	26,637.50 + 28%	137,050
208,850	372,950	46,741.50 + 33%	208,850
372,950	....	100,894.50 + 35%	372,950

If you do invest in the same property outside the IRA, then you will be subject to tax on the net operating income from the asset based upon your normal income tax rates. When you make this comparison it may well make the investment through the IRA make even more sense.

WHY SHOULD SYNDICATORS AND OTHER TAX PROFESSIONALS BE CONCERNED ABOUT THESE RULES?

Basically, in the case of a real estate syndicator, that syndicator is looking for investors to invest in a particular property. If the investment is going to involve indebtedness and some or all of the investors are likely to be IRAs or 401(k) accounts, then the existence of UBTI simply needs to be disclosed to the prospective investors. They will also likely want some explanation of the cost to their account of that indebtedness and the syndicator's plan with respect to the indebtedness, particularly if the plan is to pay off the indebtedness prior to a sale of the property.

Likewise, the real estate broker or other real estate professional needs to be aware of these rules so that if their clients are IRAs they take into account the amount of the taxable income the IRAs investing will realize from the investment. Again, while unrelated business taxable income is not fatal to an investment, it simply must be taken into account in terms of how good the investment is relative to other possible investments.

Next Chapter

Now that you have mastered the rules on what constitutes unrelated business taxable income and how to compute this, it is time for you to be exposed to Plan Asset Rules. If you will turn to the next chapter, you will explore this important and sometimes misunderstood area.

Chapter 12

Investment Through Entities: The Plan Asset Rules and Rollins and Its Offspring

Introduction

The Plan Asset Rules are technical but, nonetheless, you need to at least be aware of them as you look at investments of your IRA or 401(k) plan account through entities.

What if I Do Business With an Entity Owned by the Plan?

All the prohibited transaction rules literally deal with transactions between you or some other disqualified person and the assets of your plan. If the plan assets include, for example, ownership of less than a 50% interest in a limited liability company which in turn owns a real estate asset, the question may arise as to whether you can do business with the real estate even if you could not do business with the LLC. That's because it is only the ownership interest in the company which is the asset of the plan, not the underlying assets of the real estate.

The same rules would apply to the assets of other entities such as partnerships and corporations, but I have chosen to focus on the limited liability company simply because the use of it has become so pervasive. The LLC has become so popular because it combines elements of the corporation (unlike the partnership it does not have to have a general partner so no member is liable for the debts of the entity) and the tax attributes of a partnership. There is a pass-through of items of income and loss to the members.

Unfortunately, there is a whole set of rules dealing with this general subject called the "Plan Asset Rules." Without getting overly technical, in addition to the IRS rules, there are Department of Labor rules promulgated under Title I of ERISA (the "Employee Retirement Income Security Act of 1974"). While IRAs are not literally subject to ERISA, there is a Department of Labor ("DOL") opinion letter that states that IRAs are subject to the Plan Asset Rules. Everyone now accepts that IRAs are clearly subject to the Plan Asset Rules.

What Are the Plan Asset Rules?

As is true in many areas of the rules dealing with retirement plan investments and entities, the Plan Asset Rules are convoluted in that they start out by saying that the assets of an entity in which a qualified plan invests are not viewed as assets of the plan itself. However, they go on to carve out an exception that basically says that if a qualified plan invests in an equity interest of an entity, and that interest is neither a publicly held security nor a security issued by an investment company registered under the Investment Company Act of 1940, the plan's assets include both the equity interest **and** an undivided interest in each underlying asset of the entity unless:

(i) The entity is an operating company; or

(ii) Equity participation in the entity by plan investors is not significant.

Since most of the investments that we encounter are not investments in publicly held securities nor securities issued by an investment company registered under the Investment Company Act of 1940, the two exceptions from the general rule become crucial.

Unless you fall within one of these two exceptions to the Plan Asset Rules, your IRA or qualified plan will be regarded as owing a pro rata percentage of the underlying assets of any entity in which the plan invests equal to the plan's percentage interest in the entity. For example, if you are subject to the Plan Asset Rules and your IRA owns a 25% interest in an LLC owning a shopping center, your IRA will be treated as owning 25% of the shopping center. The upshot of this is that if you or some other disqualified person then does business with the LLC regarding the shopping center (such as someone taking a commission on the sale of the center), then this can cause you and your IRA to violate the prohibited transactions rules.

What Is the Exception for Participation not Being Significant?

Equity participation in the entity by benefit plan investors will not be significant if your IRA or other qualified plan together with other benefit plan investors owns less than 25% of any class of the entity's equity interests. "Benefit plan investors" include virtually any sort of employee benefit plan, whether or not covered by ERISA, including IRAs. In calculating this 25%, you eliminate from the total ownership of the entity any interest held by a person who has discretionary authority and control of the assets of the entity. Clearly, if you are a manager of a limited liability company in which your plan owns an interest, you get picked up within this rule. You also would likely get picked up by this rule if you were a member of the limited liability company, with some voting rights or some practical control over the entity, in which your plan is also a member.

Say, for example, you are an investor in an LLC and your IRA, together with other benefit plans, own 24% of the membership interests in the LLC. If you own 20% of the membership interest directly, then the participation by benefit plan investors is significant because the 24% held by them represents 30% of the value of the class exclusive of the 20% you own directly (i.e., 24% of 80%) and that exceeds 25%. This rule aggregates the ownership interests of all benefit plan investors even if the investors are unrelated to each other.

The Pension Protection Act of 2006 made changes in the definition of benefit plan investors under the Plan Asset Rules. However, it appears these changes only related to foreign plans or government plans. Therefore, I would assume that IRAs and 401(k)s are still subject to the Plan Asset Rules.

WHAT IS THE EXCEPTION FOR AN OPERATING COMPANY?

If you do not fall within that exception then you have to look at the exception for whether the entity is an operating company. There are three types of operating companies:

1. A basic operating company which is an entity primarily engaged, directly or through majority owned subsidiaries, in the production or sale of a product or service other than the investment of capital. This exception will be unlikely to apply in most cases.

2. A venture capital operating company which must satisfy two requirements:

   At least 50% of the entity's assets (valued at cost) must be invested in venture capital investments or derivative investments; and

   The entity must actually exercise management rights in connection with one or more of its operating company investments.

   This exception also probably does not apply to most situations.

3. The final exception is one that may apply to at least some situations, and this is the exception for a real estate operating company. To qualify as a real estate operating company, a limited liability company or other entity must meet two conditions:

   First, at least 50% of its assets (valued at cost) must be invested in real estate which is (i) managed or developed, and (ii) with respect to which such entity has the right to substantially participate directly in the management or development activities; and

Second, the entity must be directly engaged in real estate management or development activities in the ordinary course of its business.

There are a great many rules regarding this exception, together with a number of examples under the DOL Regulations.

WHY THE CONCERN WITH THE ROLLINS DECISION AND DOL OPINION 2006 - 01A?

Many people had assumed that, as long as an IRA or qualified plan owned less than 50% of an entity, it was allowable for the plan owner to do business with the entity at least as long as it did not fall within the Plan Asset Rules. However, then the Rollins decision was released in 2004. Without getting into detail on this, the IRS took a substance over form approach to say that, regardless of any of the percentage interest ownership or other rules, if the IRS felt that the owner of an IRA or plan was involved with an entity owned in part by the plan or the IRA and the plan or IRA was being benefited, then this would constitute a prohibited transaction. While many commentators feel that Rollins may not be good law, it further illustrates the danger of this whole area of doing business with your IRA or qualified plan.

Moreover, in a later opinion letter issued by the DOL, the analysis seems to generally disregard the operating company exception from the Plan Asset Rules. Given these decisions, even if you think you fall clearly within one of the exceptions, such as that for an operating company, these decisions call into question how much security you should take in that conclusion.

WHAT DOES IT MEAN AS A PRACTICAL MATTER IF AN ENTITY FALLS UNDER THE PLAN ASSETS RULES?

The practical issue becomes that the managers of the LLC are held to the same standards as are other fiduciaries with respect to the investors. If the managers reach agreement on fees and other material matters with investors before the time that the investors become members in the LLC, then this is probably okay. However, once the investors become members of the LLC, then the managers must in all cases act as fiduciaries with respect to the member IRAs.

Among other practical facts, the managers cannot utilize their own IRAs or 401(k) accounts to directly invest in the company.

NEXT CHAPTER

Now that you have plowed through the Plan Asset Rules and you are at least aware of what is going on here, the next chapter will help you deal with some of the practicalities of owning real estate in your IRA.

CHAPTER 13

Practicalities of Owning and Selling
Real Estate in Your IRA

OWNING REAL ESTATE IN YOUR IRA

INTRODUCTION

Every administrator is probably going to have a slightly different method of doing things. The key thing is to make sure that all income earned is paid to your IRA or 401(k) plan account and that all expenses are paid out of your IRA or 401(k) plan account.

PAYMENT OF ONGOING EXPENSES DIRECTLY BY YOUR IRA OR 401(K) PLAN ACCOUNT

Your administrator is likely going to want you to specifically authorize the payment of any expenses out of your IRA or 401(k) plan account. Each administrator will likely have a form for this.

The administrator probably will allow for a blanket authorization by you of any payment of ongoing expenses such as mortgage payments, homeowner's dues and the like.

PROPERTY MANAGEMENT

You can handle some of the property management functions yourself as long as you are careful to make sure that all income is remitted directly to your IRA or 401(k) plan account and that all expenses are paid out of the IRA or 401(k) plan account.

If you do choose to employ a management company, then the contract with the management company will have to be entered into by your administrator on behalf of your IRA or 401(k) plan account. In addition, the administrator likely will require some sort of a letter of acknowledgment from the property management firm that the property is owned by the IRA or 401(k) plan account and that the manager's relationship is with the administrator for such account. In other words, you can choose the property manager but the property manager's relationship has to be with the administrator of your IRA or 401(k) plan account.

The management company can pay many of the expenses of the property on behalf of your IRA or 401(k) plan account but will have to provide your administrator regular reports regarding the payments of these expenses.

SELLING REAL ESTATE HELD IN YOUR IRA

INTRODUCTION

As was the case with buying real estate, your administrator is likely to have a slightly different procedure in working through having your IRA or 401(k) plan account sell that real estate asset. You simply need to make sure you understand what the requirements of your administrator are in advance.

This should be a happy day for you because, if you have chosen wisely, then you should be able to sell the asset at a significant profit.

CHOOSING A BROKER

The first step likely will be finding a broker who will list the property for sale. Maybe you will be lucky enough to find a buyer without the services of a broker or other professional but those instances will be rare and the real estate agent or broker will earn his or her money in finding a buyer and conducting the sales process.

CONTRACT STAGE

When your broker presents you with an offer that you think is acceptable, the offer should then be reduced to a contract. You should read over the contract and, once you are satisfied with it, mark it "read and approved" and send it on to your administrator.

The administrator will then sign the offer on behalf of the IRA or 401(k) plan account. The administrator also will likely have some additional paper work whereby you authorize the sale.

Closing the Sale

You will receive a copy of the closing documents from the title company or from your attorney depending on the state where the property is located. You should review all of these for accuracy and then forward them on to your IRA or 401(k) plan account administrator marked "read and approved." The administrator will then sign anything necessary in the name of your IRA or 401(k) plan account.

Finally, make sure that the proceeds of the sale are sent (preferably by wire) directly to your IRA or 401(k) plan account administrator for the benefit of your IRA or 401(k) plan account.

Next Chapter

Now that you understand the practicalities of owning and selling a real estate asset in your IRA or 401(k) plan account, the next step in your education focuses on 401(k) plan accounts. I think you will find this very valuable reading since much of the wealth of many of us is made up in our 401(k) accounts.

Chapter 14

401(k) Plan Accounts—An Alternative to IRAs

Introduction

401(k) plans deserve separate mention because there is so much wealth tied up in 401(k) plans today. The 401(k) plan has become increasingly popular with employers as a method to encourage retirement savings by employees while minimizing the cost to the employer. My experience is that the 401(k) plan is often replacing the traditional pension plan as the retirement plan of choice at many businesses.

The reason the 401(k) plan is so popular with employers is that much of the contributions are funded by contributions of the employee. Often the employer will match funds up to a certain level, although the matching has lessened somewhat during the recession.

For example, John has a 401(k) plan account with his employer. The employer will match up to 3% of John's annual compensation if John contributes a like amount to the account. John elects to contribute 3% in order to secure the employer's matching 3% for a total of 6%. John might also have the option of contributing a larger amount such as 6% of his adjusted gross income but the employer would be required to match only 3%. John would still want to consider contributing the maximum amount even if he was not receiving a match on all of it because the amount contributed by John would be deductible and would accelerate the growth of his 401(k) plan account.

This obviously costs the employer much less than the traditional pension plan under which the employer was responsible for payments to the employee at retirement. Under the 401(k) plan the employee looks to his or her individual account maintained under the plan for retirement dollars.

Picking back up with John again, let's say that the employer's 401(k) plan has $1 million in assets but John's plan account is worth only $100,000. It is only from this $100,000 in John's plan account that he will receive distributions in retirement. The value of the total 401(k) plan of the employer is irrelevant.

WHAT IS A 401(K) PLAN?

The basics of the 401(k) plan were touched on earlier but it may be helpful to list these points again:

- A 401(k) plan is an employer-sponsored plan whereby the employee contributes funds to an account which will later be used for his or her retirement. Typically, the employer matches the employee's funds up to a certain amount to encourage the employee to make contributions to the retirement plan.

The following is a diagram that may be of help to you in visualizing the 401(k) plan and your account's place in the plan:

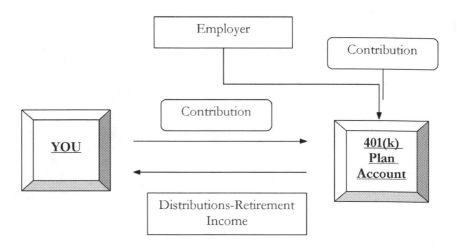

As is obvious from the diagram, both you and potentially your employer will be making contributions to the plan account maintained for you.

As we learned earlier in the example with John, each employee has a separate account under the 401(k) plan of the employer. It is only that particular account over which the employee has some control as far as investments and from which the employee receives distributions in retirement. The employee has no rights to the assets of the plan as a whole, but rather only has rights in the assets of his or her account.

Again, it is important to remember that your 401(k) plan account is separate from you.

Other important points to know:

- 401(k) plans are what are called defined contribution plans. This means that certain amounts are contributed to the plan account maintained for the individual employee and the growth of the plan account is up to the investment choices made by the employee within the range of options offered by the employer's chosen trustee or administrator. Typically, the trustee or administrator is a bank and the investment choices will be limited to specified mutual funds.

- Unlike IRAs, these plans are subject to ERISA.

- Many of the concepts I will discuss related to IRAs also apply to 401(k)s, although 401(k)s are, by their nature, not so easy to self-direct.

- The 401(k) does provide certain advantages with regard to investments generating unrelated business taxable income as discussed in more detail in an earlier chapter and below.

Investment in Real Estate

While 401(k) funds as well as IRA funds can be invested in real estate, you may find that larger employers often resist any sort of changes to their existing 401(k) plan. Most employer plans maintained with a traditional administrator allow you to invest only in stocks or bonds or an approved list of mutual funds.

You may, therefore, be faced with the prospect of not being able to invest in real estate. However, there are a number of possibilities that may allow you to invest 401(k) funds in real estate even before you leave or change jobs.

Perhaps the easiest is to simply have a change of trustee to one that allows for investments in real estate. Another alternative is, with a cooperative employer, a termination of employment followed by a rehiring so that you have a break in service allowing for a distribution out to an IRA. There may also be opportunities for in-service distributions once you have reached certain ages depending upon what your plan may provide.

Much easier is the case where you have funds from a 401(k) with a former employer. These can easily be moved into a self-directed IRA and the resulting IRA can be invested in real estate. Some of these rollovers from 401(k) plans can result in substantial IRAs.

401(k) Plans and UBTI

The 401(k) plan can be particularly advantageous with regard to investment in real estate financed in part with debt, as the typical 401(k) plan is not subject to the UBTI rules. Therefore, you generally can invest in debt-financed property through a 401(k) plan without generating unrelated business taxable income. This means a 401(k) plan is obviously a prime choice for investment in real estate where the investment is going to be financed at least in part with debt.

As discussed briefly above, most qualified plans, including 401(k) plans, are not subject to the tax on debt financed income so long as the indebtedness qualifies under the following points:

- The acquisition price for the property is fixed as of the date of purchase.

- The debt is third-party debt and not financing by the seller, a person related to the seller, or a person related to the plan. If any of these people do provide financing then it must be on "commercially reasonable terms." Because of that vagueness, it is probably best to stay away from seller or related party financing.

- Payments on the debt are not based upon the income or profits from the property.

- The property is not leased back to the seller or a person related to the seller.

- The property is not leased to a person related to the plan.

- The purchaser is not a partnership in which the plan is a partner together with taxable persons where the allocations are designed to avoid tax.

While this is quite a list of exceptions, the reality is that most real estate acquisitions by 401(k)s or qualified plans can avoid these exceptions and, therefore, avoid the tax on unrelated business taxable income related to acquisition indebtedness.

In most cases, this means that only IRAs will be really concerned about the debt-financed property rules and that 401(k) plans and other qualified plans likely will not be as concerned unless, of course, they fall within one of the exceptions that would put them back into the debt-financed income rules. If you have a 401(k) plan or other qualified plan, you simply need to analyze each real estate investment that involves debt to make sure it is not subject to these rules, or, if it is, to calculate the cost to the plan.

NEXT CHAPTER

Now that you are well versed in 401(k) plan accounts, it is time to move on to a primer about contributions and distributions with respect to IRAs. Therefore, the next chapter will just briefly summarize those rules so you will have them in mind as you pursue real estate investments.

CHAPTER 15

Overview of Contribution and Distribution Rules

INTRODUCTION

Although this book is not intended to focus on the rules regarding contributions to and distribution from IRAs and 401(k) plan accounts, I thought it would be helpful to touch on these at least briefly. You should check with your tax advisers or the Internal Revenue Service website (www.irs.gov) for more information on the contribution and distribution rules.

CONTRIBUTIONS

The rules regarding contributions to your IRA or 401(k) plan account are summarized very briefly below.

TRADITIONAL IRA

If neither you nor your spouse is covered by a qualified employer-sponsored plan, you can contribute an amount equal to your earned income up to $5,000 (whichever is less) plus an additional $1,000 contribution if you are age 50 or greater. If one of the spouses does not have earned income then that spouse can nonetheless contribute so long as the earned income of the couple is at least $10,000.

However, if you or your spouse is covered by a qualified employer-sponsored plan, then the amount you can deduct for contributions to an IRA is reduced by the contributions by the employee to a traditional 401(k) plan. I have found, as a practical matter, that most employed people are covered by 401(k)s or other qualified plans. Therefore, these people will not be able to make deductible contributions to an IRA.

Roth IRA

The contribution limits to the Roth are the same as for a regular IRA. However, unlike the traditional IRA, the contributions are not deductible. The trade off is that distributions from a Roth IRA are not taxable.

The maximum contribution limits apply regardless of how many IRAs one may have, so if one has both traditional and Roth IRAs, the maximum contribution can only be made once and must be split between the types of IRAs.

401(k)

The contribution limit for a 401(k) is $16,500 plus a catch-up contribution of $5,500 if the employee is age 50 or older. These plans often involve employer matching at least up to a certain level. The matching amounts are not compensation to the employee.

Roth 401(k)

There are Roth 401(k)s and, like the Roth IRA, the contributions are not tax deductible.

DISTRIBUTIONS

The rules regarding distributions from your IRA or 401(k) plan account are summarized very briefly below.

Traditional IRA

You must begin to take distributions in the year after you turn 70½. The distributions are taxable and they may be subject to a 10% penalty if you begin taking distributions prior to obtaining age 59½. You can begin taking distributions without penalty at age 59½. In addition, there are a handful of exceptions allowing earlier withdrawals without penalty. If you are disabled, you can use the withdrawal to pay medical expenses in excess of 7.5% of your adjusted gross income or you can use the distribution to buy health insurance.

Roth IRA

Distributions from a Roth IRA are generally not taxable to the recipient.

401(k)

The rules for distributions from a 401(k) plan account are similar to those with respect to distributions from an IRA in that you must begin taking distributions in the year after you turn 70½, and you can begin taking distributions without penalty upon attaining age 59½. Again, the distributions are taxable to you as taken.

Roth 401(k)

Distributions from a Roth 401(k) are generally not taxable to the recipient.

Some Practical Tips on Distributions

The following may be of help to you in dealing with distributions from an IRA or 401(k) invested in real estate:

- If minimum distributions are required from an IRA containing real estate, any valuation needed for purposes of the minimum distribution calculations is up to the account owner to obtain. I understand it does not need to be a formal appraisal, but it needs to be something that would stand up to scrutiny. Property tax assessments are not sufficient, but a real estate broker or someone knowledgeable about property in the area can provide a sufficient valuation (in either case the amount of any mortgage debt is deducted).

- If distributions are required and real estate is the only asset, then required distributions can be made of an undivided interest in the property. Ideally you would have a property generating sufficient cash flow to meet the required distributions because distributing slices of the property is messy from a practical standpoint.

Conclusion

This is only a very brief summary of the contribution and distribution rules. There has been plenty written on contribution and distribution rules, and I'd encourage you to check with your own tax advisers and the Internal Revenue Service website.

Next Chapter

Congratulations! You only have one more chapter to go. As much as I believe in real estate investment by IRA and 401(k) plan accounts, there are some drawbacks to that investment. The next chapter focuses on those drawbacks. Because of the opportunity for abuse in the case of an LLC wholly owned by an IRA, this is a subject which gets a considerable amount of scrutiny from the regulatory authorities.

CHAPTER 16

Issues in the Investments in Real Estate by IRAs and 401(k) Plan Accounts

INTRODUCTION

While this is a fertile market for syndicators and other real estate professionals seeking capital for transactions, there are a couple of limitations that come with the investment by IRAs and 401(k) plan accounts.

The first is the Plan Asset Rules and the second is the requirement for an annual valuation. The third issue, related to investments in real estate by IRAs, but not generally by 401(k) plan accounts, involves unrelated business taxable income.

PLAN ASSET RULES

As discussed in an earlier chapter, whenever you have IRAs holding at least 25% of an investment such as a membership interest in an LLC (subject to the adjustment for investment by and controlled by the owner of the IRA) then the investment by the IRAs become subject to the Plan Asset Rules. There are various repercussions to this.

As discussed earlier, there are ways to deal with these rules such that syndicators and other real estate professionals should not discount the idea of pursuing a transaction or pursuing IRAs and 401(k)s to invest in a transaction simply because they are afraid that they will become subject to the Plan Asset Rules.

Annual Valuation

An annual valuation needs to be prepared on real estate assets owned by an IRA. The same rules apply to an LLC which is owned in part by IRAs. The need for the valuation is particularly acute in the case of an LLC wholly owned by an IRA.

This valuation must be of a special quality by an independent party that the IRA administrator will be comfortable with should the Internal Revenue Service ever examine their files. The cost of such valuations will ultimately be borne by the IRAs investing in real estate assets.

At least some administrators are saying they reserve the right to distribute out an investment in real estate by an IRA if the annual valuations are not provided.

Unrelated Business Taxable Income

An investment in real estate using debt at least raises the possibility of there being unrelated business taxable income. This can result in at least part of the income from an investment becoming taxable to an IRA. 401(k) accounts generally are exempted from these rules except in rare instances. All of this was discussed in an earlier chapter.

Conclusion

Congratulations for having made your way through this entire book. If you have read it carefully, you are now equipped to go out and pursue real estate investments in your IRA or 401(k) plan account.

As you will have already learned from the Introduction, I believe very strongly in IRA and 401(k) investment in real estate as a means of increasing your wealth. I have recently made an investment using personal funds as well as funds from my IRA and my wife's 401(k), and I am pursuing other real estate investments for my IRA and my wife's IRA and 401(k). I think if you look around, you will find real bargains in the real estate area and I highly recommend that you give serious consideration to such an investment. I also recommend that with interest rates as low as they are, you look at partnering with your IRA and possibly borrowing some money personally to augment the funds in your IRA (you learned earlier that you cannot use the asset being purchased in part by your IRA as security for the loan but you can use other assets such as your principal residence as security). I have recently done that and highly recommend that you consider it.

Perhaps the best advice I can give you is that as you develop your skills in this area, communicate as much as possible with the administrator of your IRA or 401(k) plan account and take his or her advice in pursuing real estate investments.

Good hunting!